Library of Congress Cataloging in Publication Data

Dourlein, Pieter.
Inside North Pole.
(Classics of World War II. The secret war)
Reprint. Originally published: London: W. Kimber, 1953.
1. Dourlein, Pieter. 2. World War, 1939-1945—Secret service—Great
Britain. 3. Spies—Great Britain—Biography. 4. World War, 1939-1945—
Personal narratives, Dutch. 5. World War, 1939-1945—Underground
movements—Netherlands. 6. Prisoners of war—Netherlands—Biogra-
phy. 7. World War, 1939-1945—Prisoners and prisons, German.
I. Title. II. Series.
D810.S8D57 1988   940.54'86'41   88-29494
ISBN 0-8094-7262-7
ISBN 0-8094-7263-5 (lib. bdg.)

INSIDE NORTH POLE

INSIDE NORTH POLE

A SECRET AGENT'S STORY

by

PIETER DOURLEIN

WILLIAM KIMBER
LONDON

First published in England in 1953 by

WILLIAM KIMBER AND CO. LIMITED

46 Wilton Place, London, S.W.1

Translated by

F. G. Renier and Anne Cliff

MADE AND PRINTED IN GREAT BRITAIN BY PURNELL AND SONS, LTD.
PAULTON (SOMERSET) AND LONDON

Publisher's Note

A FULL account of the initiation and development of Operation North Pole from the German side is contained in *London Calling North Pole* by Colonel H. J. Giskes, former Chief of German Military Counter-Intelligence in Holland, Belgium and northern France.

Contents

CHAPTER I

FIVE MAY DAYS

MAY 10th, 1940, early morning. The Dutch destroyer *Jan van Galen* was anchored off the northern Dutch naval station Den Helder. She was straining at her anchor-chains, pitching and heaving on a grey and turbulent sea. On the near horizon the first light of dawn was slanting on the glistening line of sand-dunes. The air was alive with the incessant drone of aeroplanes.

Armed with a pot of paint and a brush, I was clinging to a two-plank stage slung against the side of the dancing ship, covering the bright red, white and blue markings of what had been a neutral vessel with a layer of grey paint. For Holland was no longer a neutral country. We had been at war for some hours.

The *Jan van Galen* had left Surabaya in early April. The voyage had been far from pleasant; we had had to pass through more than one theatre of war, and a variety of mines had been among the lesser perils. The crew were all professional navy people who had spent from two to four years in East Indian waters. Neither they nor the many friends who had waved them farewell had imagined that their leave-taking would, in many cases, be for ever.

On May 7th we had entered the harbour of Nieuwediep by Den Helder. A mound of trunks and kitbags lay ready for taking ashore; practically every member of the crew had amassed as many presents as possible for wives,

[11]

children, parents, friends and fiancées. But, alas, we had hardly arrived before the news went round that all leave of absence had been stopped and that shore leave did not extend beyond the limits of Den Helder. How we envied those fortunates whose people lived in the town; the others wandered from café to café, disconsolately swilling beer. We had had these alarums before. Done to annoy, that was all.

And then, some time during the evening of the 9th, the order came: All personnel on board. Patrols went through town calling at homes and cafés. Shortly after midnight the first confused tidings of the invasion reached us. By three o'clock the *Jan van Galen* had left harbour and was anchored in the roadstead. At half-past four we had our first alert. As the fire of ack-ack batteries and the hum of aeroplanes filled our ears, the captain, Lieutenant-Commander Pinke, called us all to muster aft.

I was twenty-two, Leading Seaman Pieter Dourlein. And here I was, slapping murky grey paint over the gay red, white and blue. It struck me as a symbolic action: the fog of war spreading over my native country. But I saw no reason to be unduly depressed. High above our heads flew the pennant of active service, a signal that had not graced a Dutch man-of-war for some time now. It was a fine, new pennant, and it filled us with courage. Were we not all well trained and of excellent physique? It did not occur to the crew that modern warfare held many surprises in store, or that the wonderful equipment so familiar to us would prove to be of so little avail against new methods of attack.

It was broad daylight by now, and from the harbour came a tug bringing us an extra supply of munitions. I was with the gun-crews amidships, and before long our anti-aircraft guns were in action against some Junkers 52 which were dropping magnetic mines. The *Jan van Galen*'s next order was to sail for the Hook of Holland, and we set out at full speed, following a course some seven miles off shore. As we were passing Kijkduin our look-out spotted three planes on the sandy beach, one of them still taxi-ing along, large glittering objects: Junkers 52 again. The captain gave his orders, guns were sighted, and a few rounds from our 12-cm. guns sent at least two of them up in flames amid loud cheering from our crew. So that was war, was it? In our blissful ignorance our mood rapidly veered to overconfidence. For none of us had yet heard a real bomb whistling down.

Imagine our surprise when we were told that we were going to sail up the New Waterway to Rotterdam to lend support to the land forces then engaged in fierce hand-to-hand fighting. This did not sound too good to us, for every sailor knows that a warship is particularly vulnerable in a narrow channel. The ship cannot be manœuvred and she becomes the helpless prey of any well-aimed bomb or aerial torpedo. But these were our orders from The Hague. Repeated enquiries were made to have these unbelievable instructions confirmed—but, yes, these were the orders, and orders are given to be obeyed. It was clear that they were not to the captain's liking; his own instructions showed that he was none too happy about our prospects, for before we entered the New Waterway he had all combustibles, explosives and acid containers slung in nets over the side.

At about three in the afternoon we passed the Hook. The shore was lined with cheering crowds, as if they were at a naval display. Not even the air escort was lacking; the only objection to the aircraft was that they were

German bombers. Before we had reached Maassluis there were a fair number of them immediately overhead, but at so formidable a height that there was no point in firing at them. At one moment we counted twenty. And suddenly down they swooped, in a dive-bombing attack. Bullets, bombs and shells hurtled round us in a hail that pattered on the water, on the decks, against the sides of the ship. The sun went on shining, and surprisingly one found oneself working away for dear life. I caught myself leaning over the rail of the bridge, watching a bomb scrape along the ship's side and disappear into the unresisting water. Oddly interesting.

Our anti-aircraft fire was active but ineffectual. It was soon obvious that our equipment was totally out of date for effectively opposing the German war machine. After a very few shots, our old 40-mm. guns would jam and we would work feverishly with a wooden mallet to put them right.

Though the *Jan van Galen* did not receive a direct hit, she sprang some leaks and began slowly to settle. The captain made a valiant attempt to enter Rotterdam harbour so that he could come alongside a quay, but the steering-gear was damaged and failed to respond. The captain roared with fury as we nearly sank a large Rhine-barge in our ineffectual flounderings. We made the shore and did our best to keep the ship on an even keel by means of cables and hawsers, but one after the other they parted.

One dead and a dozen wounded were carried ashore and as many portable weapons as possible were taken off. As a final gesture our pennant was hauled down. Then Her Majesty's destroyer *Jan van Galen* slipped away and sank. It was like a funeral. We all stood and watched as at a graveside, except that we were extremely vocal. Why had those stupid fools sent us into this death-trap? Why had they not left us out in the open sea where we belonged?

The German bombers had carried out their task efficiently. Their droning died away as they withdrew, and the ensuing silence was strangely eerie. But that was merely a pause. For us total war was only just beginning.

The members of the crew were split up into various groups. I became one of Captain Schuiling's men. Schuiling had a succession of the most impossible tasks to perform and lived in his clothes, day and night. He could often be seen driving through town in the hot sun, the perspiration running down from under his helmet.

One of his jobs was to man a post by the railway station near the Exchange. He had also to hunt parachutists. Then he was told to storm the Maas Station and clear it with bayonets. Night was drawing on, it was growing cold, and it was as silent as in peace-time. For three hours we lay stretched on the cobblestones in mingled anxiety and expectation. At last the order to move came, and we crept up to the station. But before a shot had been fired we discovered that the station was still safely in the possession of our infantry. Safely and soundly—for they were all fast asleep, exhausted. That, at any rate, was how we found them. We grinned a bit on both sides; it might well have been a tragic blood-bath.

Before long there was considerable cursing and swearing, for it was becoming apparent to the meanest intelligence that something was wrong somewhere. Far too many impossible orders were being given; far too little information was being passed on. And at some point co-ordination and direction were at fault. The Dutch forces in Rotterdam, unable to see the background of the fighting in which they were involved, were being harried and harassed. Soldiers and sailors, they fought on, wherever and whenever told to do so, but the enemy was always stronger and appeared in the most unexpected places. We were waging a hopeless fight against ignorance and treachery.

On Whit Sunday I found myself entrenched, with some six or seven others, near a bridge by an eye hospital that had been badly damaged in an air attack. The street was littered with the dead and dying, who were being tended and carried away by Red Cross personnel. Over the scene lay a pall of dust and smoke, and I could hear the crackle of burning wood. A couple of Red Cross men came rushing over to us: "Please, come quickly. There's an unexploded bomb over there—will you deal with it?" Well, we could hardly say no. We were the armed forces and supposed to know it all. All right, we'd come and have a look. And there, in a little hollow among the scattered cobblestones, lay a steel bomb, a hundred-pounder, carefully manufactured in a German factory, and filled with enough high explosive to blow us all to kingdom come. There it lay for all to see. Not one of us felt like tackling it. Funny that we should clap eyes on a German bomb before ever seeing one of our own.

We went and sat down by the side of the road and drew lots with handfuls of pebbles: even—odd—even. A friend and I were unlucky and got the odd numbers. "Oh well," I said, "remember us to the others when you get there, will you?"

We picked up the bomb. Nothing happened. We tenderly carried it to the nearby canal and dropped it in. The water splashed us. That was all. And then we discovered that our knees were gently knocking together. The worst of it was that there wasn't a drink to be had for miles. We decided that we would have preferred to face a bayonet attack.

Those five May days of the first phase of Holland at war went by in a gloomy and confused regularity of exhaustion, death, destruction and impotent fury. The fury remained after the rest had passed. It was a fury that reached its zenith as, on May 14th, I watched the German squadrons appear above Rotterdam and calmly, purposefully and mercilessly bomb the inner city into a heap of smouldering ruins.

We were just outside the town and saw it all as if watching a film. Sound came through indistinctly. Of the bombs we heard but the faintest whistle and their explosions were muffled thuds. Even the scream of the dive-bombers was less loud than the anxious calls of the frightened birds and the curses of my companions. A dense column of smoke was rising high into the sky.

When the worst was over, our section decided to go back to town and see what help we could give. We could hardly make our way against the tide of people fleeing from the stricken area. Many streets were impassable as the flames leapt from house to house and across the narrow pavements. The film had become reality—a ghastly reality of fire and blood. Rotterdam was emptying in a compact human stream: well-dressed business men, workmen in shirt-sleeves and in overalls, hysterically weeping women with infants in their arms, small children, lost and crying, all trying to escape from the raging inferno under its pall of smoke. And everywhere the silent dead and the moaning wounded.

Before long, bugles were sounding the call to rally. We hurried to our posts, imagining that we were being assembled to launch a major assault. Back we went, pushing our way through the crowds, filled with a wrathful heroism and a thirst for revenge. And on arrival we were told that it was all over. Our resistance was broken.

We were to lay down arms and wait for the Germans to take over. It chilled our blood. Surely it couldn't be true—and even if it were, we wouldn't give in. Rotterdam was still blazing unchecked.

I met some of my friends from the *Jan van Galen* who, like myself, did not feel like obeying such orders. We refused to submit so tamely. We decided to carry light but useful weapons, make for the coast and try to cross over to England. We got to Scheveningen, along roads full of dispirited soldiery. Scheveningen harbour teemed with life. Our hopes flared up. There were some trawlers, all ready to sail, which suited us very well. But the skippers didn't feel like taking the risk. They stood there, chewing tobacco and shaking their heads. A moment ago, they said, a trawler full of refugees had left the harbour and they had watched it hit a magnetic mine. The whole harbour was full of mines. Suicide to sail, they said.

Night was falling. The sea was as calm and smooth as an inland lake. Not a ship was in sight. We turned away and made for The Hague and, arrived there, called at the headquarters of the navy. There was still one officer at his post, his uniform spotless and uncreased. He was amazed to see us carrying arms and lost his temper. "Why haven't you laid down your arms? Haven't you been given orders? We have capitulated, and if the Germans, who are expected any moment, find you, they'll shoot us all at sight as *francs-tireurs*. And they'd be entitled to." And so on.

Then reaction set in. We were suddenly desperately tired. We had hardly slept for the past four nights. Street-lamps were alight again and the café terraces were thronged with silent people. It was a warm spring evening. We walked through The Hague like sleepwalkers, and the next morning we woke up in the stables of the old

Alexandra cavalry barracks. How we got there we did not remember.

A few moments later the first German staff cars entered the town. The noise of their engines echoed from the walls of the Palace of Peace.

CHAPTER 2

A TWO-SEATER CANOE

ON JULY 15th, 1940, I was taken off active service and put on half-pay after I had declined to join the Reconstruction Services. Slowly I crossed the barrack square, thinking of my possessions which were now all lying at the bottom of Rotterdam harbour. This was the most wretched homecoming I had had.

I decided to go and see my parents, who lived in the south, on the Isle of Walcheren. I had not seen them for well over three years, and, though I was delighted to see them again, our meeting was not as joyful as I had so often pictured it when I was in Surabaya. A shadow lay over it. One of my brothers, who was also in the navy, had been posted as missing. I could only hope that he had escaped safely to England.

Life ashore, in these altered circumstances, was not very satisfactory. I was used to a free life out at sea, one of a small, well-knit community of men. Ashore, on Walcheren, I felt cooped up and depressed. I could not forget standing on the wall of Scheveningen harbour on the day of capitulation with liberty apparently within reach, yet eluding our grasp.

After a few months at home playing the part of the prodigal son, I began to ponder the problem of getting to England. I listened first to rumours. There was always supposed to be someone, just round the corner, who knew how to get you out, but as soon as you tried to follow it up the rumour proved to be utterly baseless. Just talk. And I realized that the only thing to do was to rely on my own initiative and go ahead. I passed some time, not unpleasantly, cutting German telephone lines and harassing Dutch Nazis before a plan occurred to me—to offer my services to the river police. This should afford a chance of working my way in and laying hands on a boat.

This scheme fell through, for I was called up to serve in the State police, the *maréchaussée*. For a short time I thought of going into hiding, and then it occurred to me that as a policeman I should probably have a greater freedom of movement than as an ordinary civilian. I reported at the camp at Hoog Soeren, where I was soon immersed in the study of dry-as-dust laws and police regulations. I loathed it, but felt it was the price I had to pay for the chance of freedom.

For four or five months I walked around in a dark-blue uniform, looking every inch a bad policeman. My pro-German superiors made their dislike of me very clear. And then came my chance. In May 1941 I came into contact with Sergeant-Major Buitenhuis from Rotterdam, who turned out to have a boat hidden away, waiting only for a reliable companion to make the crossing to England. Soon after meeting him I failed to resist the temptation of giving a Dutch Nazi a sound thrashing in my official capacity, which meant that the time had come for me to make myself scarce and go underground, or, to put it the Dutch way, to dive under. I went and joined Buitenhuis.

He was a likeable fellow, a year older than myself, and his craft was hidden off the Oude Maas in a canal on an island, south of Rotterdam. The moment I clapped eyes on it I burst into a roar of laughter. "Jesus, that's barely a canoe. It's not seaworthy. If we don't happen to pick a dead calm we shall be food for fishes!"

Buitenhuis, who knew nothing of the sea, looked at me with suspicion. Was I yellow? "It's a two-seater canoe. What's wrong with that? We've got to take a risk."

It was hardly a risk, it was a gamble; but he was right. "O.K. We'll go. At least we'll have a try."

From Barendrecht we went to Den Briel, or Brielle as it is known to the English, about twenty miles away. And that little trip took us three days—or, to be more accurate, three nights, for we could paddle only during the hours of darkness; during the daytime we had to hide in the reeds, for we were in the heart of a prohibited area. My brand-new policeman's uniform, which I was still wearing in the thought that it might come in useful, was soon covered in mud.

We paddled as silently as we could. It was chilly on the water, though the sun shone all day from a cloudless sky. Occasionally we would come upon a little bank of mist, and, chilly as it was, we were sweating like horses. As the vague silhouette of a farm loomed up we drew in. Morning was just breaking as I went ashore, carefully picking my way through the marshy meadows and zigzagging between the ruminating cows.

I was about fifty yards from what I had assumed to be a farm when I was brought up short, petrified by what I saw. It wasn't a farm at all but a German searchlight post with a sentry standing by a clump of willows. I could just make out the dull gleam of his buttons, belt and helmet. Silently, imperceptibly, I began to slither backwards, keeping my eye on that sentry. Bent double, I tried to use the cows as cover, but the animals, hopeful of food and company, began to display a friendly interest in me, snorting and waggling their flanks. I had to get away—and suddenly the ground seemed to open under my feet. I fell backwards into a ditch. I scrambled to my feet again, wiping away the duckweed from my eyes, and peered in the direction of the sentry. The man had not moved. I crawled on hands and knees back to the canoe, where my companion had stretched himself out and was leisurely smoking a cigarette in his cupped hand. When he caught sight of me, muddy and dripping with water and duckweed, he gave a soundless laugh. After I had told him what had happened, he said, "Well, we'd better get moving, or else you'll catch your death of cold."

We made Brielle, and again I managed to get ashore and enter the town. I called on a man named Zabel, a stoker I had known on board the *Jan van Galen*, and his people gave me every possible help. They told me that if our attempt failed and we were not caught we should come straight back to them, for Zabel could lay hands on a good motor-launch which was being used in raising the *J. P. Coen* at the entrance to Ymuiden harbour. Zabel was employed on the work as a diver and would doubtless give us all the assistance he could.

It was a bit late now, we felt. Better to go on with what we were doing.

On the fourth night conditions seemed favourable; at any rate, it was dark enough. There was a strong current in the estuary to carry us out, and hardly had we started before we passed a German patrol vessel, anchored in midstream. The look-out failed to observe us; soundlessly we drifted past, towards freedom—or that was what we thought until we ran straight into a kind of boom. We had to get out of the canoe and, standing up to our shoulders in water, lift the craft over it. After a couple of hours of frantic, if silent, paddling we crossed the bar and were out at sea. We started the outboard motor.

At first all went well. The sea was calm. Buitenhuis

even began to whistle. But our triumph was short-lived. As both of us were ignorant of the nature of the local channels, we had blindly set a course away from the land. It had not yet begun to grow light before we were startled by the sound of crashing waves, and I guessed that we were off a sandbank. We tried to change our course, but it was too late. In a moment we were in the sweep of the surge and our tiny craft became unmanageable and inevitably capsized. We could have wept with rage. We clung to the canoe, now at the mercy of the waves, and drifted. After at least five hours of this we were cast ashore—whereabouts we had no notion. It turned out to be on the beach of the South Holland island of Voorne-Putten, the very island we had left so few hours before. Chilled to the bone, on the point of exhaustion, we clambered on to the dry sand and found ourselves amid German posts and batteries.

For a few moments we lay stretched out on the sandy beach, panting as if we had been running. Our clothes were sticking to us, and we were back where we started, only worse off. We were beginning to realize exactly how awkward our situation was. Not only had we failed to make our escape but we had landed ourselves in a trap.

We did not utter a word, but, as if by arrangement, we got to our feet, crouched, and sprinted across the sands. Before long we were covered in sand; it stuck to our faces, hands and clothes, and we began to look as if we were made of sandpaper. Once we had reached the dunes we found some cover behind a gorse-bush. We dropped to the ground in a hollow where the early-morning sun seemed to have some warmth. Our cigarettes were soaked, as were our matches—as if it mattered. We made a vain effort to tidy ourselves, and, as we were beginning to shiver, we decided to brazen it out and try to get back to

Brielle. But we had gone no more than a few paces before we suddenly found ourselves face to face with a German patrol. It was so sudden that there would have been no point in trying to run for it, so we walked straight up to the Germans, pretending we were overjoyed to see them.

The German N.C.O. looked us up and down and was astute enough to realize that there was undoubtedly some connection between us and a stranded canoe that his men had found a short time ago. But he was not clever enough to draw his conclusions in silence, and, being a German, he was vaguely impressed by my police-officer's uniform, however rumpled it looked.

Taking this cue, I began boldly to improvise. Yes, it was our canoe. Glad they'd found it. I was in the State police, and my companion was a trainee. But we had had bad luck and our canoe had capsized. I was so pleased we had met the patrol, for we had lost our bearings. Were we in the right direction for Brielle?

The N.C.O. was not all that backward, unfortunately. He took us to the post and we were taken before his commanding officer. I clicked my heels, in so far as the sodden heels of my uniform boots would click, and proceeded to elaborate my fairy-tale. To my surprise, he swallowed it. We were given cigarettes and told to go on our way and report at a German post by a certain bridge. We departed, grateful, especially for the information about the post, which we must obviously avoid at all costs. We circumvented all dangers and arrived at Brielle, pleased at not even having had to give our names. We called at the Zabel house again and were advised to get into touch with our friend Zabel at Ymuiden—if we still felt like making another attempt. By the time we had been provided with a welcome meal and had restored our clothes to a semblance of order our courage had revived.

That night we took a local train to Rotterdam. We had decided that we had, at any rate, gained some experience and should not set out again without a better plan. We thought we had better hide another week and see what could then be done. And in the middle of the night we arrived at the house of Buitenhuis's parents. It was something of a shock to these poor people, for they had thought we had long since made our escape and were safely in England. We took a couple of days' rest before seeking our contact at Ymuiden.

I made use of this pause to travel down to Zeeland to see my parents and also to make certain arrangements. I went by train and had an uneventful journey, but early the next morning there was a telephone call from Rotterdam. It was a warning. Buitenhuis had been arrested. The Germans had found his military papers containing his name and address on the beach and, realizing that they had been tricked, had gone straight to the address and had found him there. It was obvious to me that before long Buitenhuis would be forced to tell them about me. Hurriedly I packed my police uniform away and put on civilian clothes. A quarter of an hour later I had left home and was on my way to the Brabant town of Roosendaal.

In the train I sat between two somnolent commercial travellers and had plenty of time to reflect. How safe we had felt! They had not even asked our names, and then chance had caused my companion to drop his pay-book with all particulars practically on their doorstep. The passing landscape lay smooth, green and fertile under a mild June sun. The commercial travellers were engaged in aimless chat. What was I to do, I wondered. I must make my way to Ymuiden, but by this time both State police and the German military would have circularized my particulars and both would be looking for me. I must leave nothing to chance. Better keep a sharp look-out on arriving at Roosendaal, where I had to change for Rotterdam. As the train drew in I observed that there was a remarkable number of Dutch police and German military police on the station. Not too healthy, and I must avoid risks. I let my fellow travellers get out first, taking my time in reaching down my suitcase from the rack. Then I boldly made for the door on the wrong side and crossed the tracks. Facing me was a railway van, its sliding doors slightly ajar. I dived in, suitcase and all, and pulled the doors to behind me.

Peering through the chink, I could see that all travellers were having their papers subjected to a careful scrutiny by both Dutch and German officials. As I was beginning to wonder what my next move should be, a jolt warned me that my goods train was leaving the station. The passengers from the Middelburg train on which I had travelled were still being checked. Should I jump out? That would be suicidal. Creaking and groaning, my goods train was gathering speed. Which way? North! We were going to Rotterdam. I had been lucky, and I sat down on my bag and waited. Drawing a cigarette paper from one pocket, some shag from another, I set to work rolling myself a cigarette. A gentle spring breeze fanned me. Things weren't so bad after all.

CHAPTER 3

THE GREEN COASTLINE

"NOT IN the canoe class, as you can see!" my former shipmate Zabel remarked with a grin.

"Not quite," I replied, as we stood looking at the grey naval launch that bobbed gently on the ripple of Ymuiden harbour. Everything had gone smoothly so far. I had been able to leave the goods train at Rotterdam unobserved and had succeeded in boarding a passenger train for Ymuiden, again without being noticed. Zabel was prepared to be helpful about my schemes.

"No, it certainly isn't a canoe. It's a heavy boat, and you'll have to do a good bit of rowing before you get outside the harbour."

The harbour was indeed alive with German craft, and it would plainly be out of the question to make use of the engine before passing the harbour mouth. To do so would be crying out for attention. The element of risk and uncertainty, whatever was devised, was considerable and no precautions could eliminate it.

"I can tell you," Zabel continued, as if he had followed my unspoken thoughts, "I'm not a coward, generally speaking, but honestly it's not the sort of job I'd care to tackle. Your chances are about one in five. Who's going with you?"

"I don't know yet." I was surprised at my own calmness. "I'm sure to come across one or two takers."

We stepped into the launch, cast off the ropes and

went for a spin round the harbour. I soon learned how to handle the engine, which was capable of about ten knots. And this was about the only ray of sunshine, for the amount of German activity we saw during our trial spin made me think that Zabel's estimate of one in five was on the optimistic side. But I had to go on with my plans. Zabel and I agreed that the best opportunity would be in three nights' time, and the best plan for me was to hide in a larger craft that was moored alongside the launch until the moment of starting. Zabel would see to it that the fuel tank was full and that there was a pair of oars on board.

Now I had to find a crew. I went to Ysselmonde, where I met a friend in the resistance movement and asked him for two men capable of rowing. Can do. I could rely on getting K. de Korver from Vlaardingen and J. A. den Ouden from Ysselmonde. Incidentally, did I know that, an hour after I had left home, there had been a raid on my parents' house? That everything had been searched and that the searchers had taken away a photograph of me? And that the Roosendaal check had indeed been laid on to catch me? An honour, wasn't it? I'd better take extra care, for all police patrols were bound to be on the look-out for me.

I met my travel companions, and we agreed to go to Ymuiden, each under his own steam, and meet at six o'clock that evening. We would be warmly dressed and well provided with sandwiches. I was to procure a Dutch flag, a pocket compass and a powerful torch—for signalling when we had reached England.

But we weren't there yet. On the day for setting out there was a strong west wind blowing straight from the sea into the harbour mouth, a wind too strong to row against. And then I discovered that in actual fact neither

De Korver nor Den Ouden could row at all. The former had admittedly been at sea before the war, but as a barber in a merchantman, which meant that he was better at wielding a shaving-brush than an oar. I pointed out the grim reality of the dangers we might run into, but the two men were firm in their determination to embark. And what about the rowing? They'd learn soon enough, they thought.

We spent June 17th playing cards and smoking, with occasional attempts to get some sleep. We all pretended a fine optimism, but it rang hollow even in our own ears. We were plainly in the grip of an attack of the jitters. The minutes crept on; time was moving, but only just. Towards nightfall we made for the harbour. We found the key of the cabin of the larger craft on the quay where we had arranged for Zabel to hide it. We scrambled into the small cabin and spent some more hours in nerve-racking inactivity, for we would not be able to set out before midnight—five hours yet to go. I at least had something to do, though not much. I was engaged in tying rags round the oars and the thole-pins to deaden the noise of rowing, for that was our major worry. With two expert oarsmen there would have been less of a problem, but with a couple of novices nothing could be taken for granted. I was in charge, and I felt my responsibility weighing heavily upon me.

When darkness had fallen I reconnoitred. The harbour seemed very peaceful, no signs of any activity, nothing but an occasional snatch of German song and the steady sound of wind and wave beyond the harbour—the sea, a hundred and fifty miles of which we had to cross. My nerves were by now tormenting me. England suddenly seemed farther away than the moon. Wasn't the whole plan ridiculous? Less than a hundred yards away from where we were hiding was a guard-post, with or without a look-out, who could tell? But the night was pitch-black, the wind was favourable for carrying sound away. That was some consolation, I'd have to bank on that. I put my hand in my pocket, and the feel of my service revolver gave me confidence. They wouldn't take me alive, my friend in my pocket would see to that.

One o'clock. Not a sound to be heard. In a whisper I gave the order to board the launch. And no noise. Not a sound! One careless step and we were lost. My companions took off their shoes and tiptoed on stockinged feet. I sat at the helm, the oars were placed in position, and very slowly, very carefully, we almost drifted to the other side of the harbour. I steered the boat as well as I could to the shadow of a jetty and, ridiculous as it was, gave my companions a whispered rowing lesson. It was preposterous—a rowing lesson within a hundred and fifty yards of an armed German sentry.

After about half an hour we set out in earnest. We had to be outside the harbour mouth well before the break of day or else our doom was sealed. I knew that the island in the harbour was well guarded, and I decided to cross the harbour and hug the northern pier, making for the sea close beneath it. The starlight was bright enough for us to see the glint of German helmets and rifles on the harbour island.

My two oarsmen were fortunately improving with practice and were working like galley slaves, following my whispered instructions to the letter. All was going well, though we were moving with painful slowness. Under the lee of the northern pier we could at intervals hear the heavy tread and the booming voices of the German sentries pacing their beats.

Though I insisted on my companions having frequent rests, their hands were soon severely blistered, but they clenched their teeth and persevered. We had reached a a point when to return would have been as dangerous as to go on. As we got farther away the chance of a marauding British plane rousing activity was lessening and with it the chance of our being caught in the beam of a sweeping searchlight. Yet we were moving too slowly, for we were still within earshot of the island, and in the east I could see the first ruddy glow of dawn. In an hour it would be light.

We held a council of war, though there was not much to be said. There was only one thing to do—start the engine and hope for the best. Softly the engine began to splutter—it sounded like swearing in church. I was in a cold sweat. At any moment we could expect a searchlight and a rain of bullets. But nothing happened, and we slid out between the pierheads, out into the open sea. Just at that moment an aeroplane roared overhead, and in the half-light of dawn a Heinkel 115 swooped over us. Would it . . .? No, it went on its way. Had the pilot taken us for a fishing craft, or had he not seen us at all? When we were two or three miles out at sea I put the engine full speed ahead, and on we sped towards freedom.

My companions had forgotten all about their blisters. De Korver burst into tears and insisted on shaking me by the hand. "Steady on," I said. "We haven't made it yet."

We smoked cigarettes. We hadn't had a smoke for at least five hours and the tenseness of our nerves demanded the release of a cigarette. A fresh, salty breeze blew in our faces, the sea was smooth and catching the gleams of the first rays of the morning sun. We inhaled our smoke, gazing back at the coast, which was growing clearer against the eastern sky.

Indeed we weren't there yet. Before long we sighted some fishing craft. Admittedly they were Dutch, but we knew that there were sure to be some Germans or Dutch Nazis on board, and we thought it safer to make a wide sweep, though it meant going a good way off our course. Nine o'clock, and we could still see the coastline, however dimly. And nine o'clock was the hour at which the loss of our launch was likely to be noticed. Anxiously we scanned the sea astern, but no German speedboat appeared, though time and time again our imaginations manufactured one from the sunny haze that now covered the water. Slowly and mercifully the last outline of our fatherland dissolved and we knew ourselves the only living beings within the wide green circle of our horizon.

We got out our sandwiches and greedily sank our teeth in them; never had war-time bread tasted so delicious. Together with the slices of smoked bacon provided for us by the black market, we had what seemed to us a banquet. The engine was purring away and we were making satisfactory headway; I was steering by the sun, for my small pocket compass was not much use. I was aiming for Lowestoft, which was due west of Ymuiden, our starting-point.

De Korver and Den Ouden stretched themselves out in the bottom of the launch and began discussing their plans—what they were going to do in England.

Our relief at having slipped through the narrow meshes of the German net did not leave us carefree for long. After a while we saw a grey object floating in the water not far off our course, the body of a German air-force lieutenant in an advanced state of putrefaction. We could not bring ourselves to take it in tow, or even to search it for papers, but we did remove its Luger pistol from its holster. It was a lugubrious incident which sharply reminded us that we were on no pleasure trip. Though every turn of the propellers was taking us nearer freedom and putting us further beyond the reach of possible pursuit, we still had a considerable distance to cover, and we were soon made aware that there were factors that we had not reckoned with.

About midday the engine, which had been going at maximum speed for a good many hours, began to show signs of fatigue; it was beginning to get hot, and I decided to give it half an hour's rest. And there was another thing. Zabel had assured me that there would be enough fuel in the tank for us to reach England, but I knew that in our efforts to avoid the fishing craft we had lengthened our route considerably. Those manœuvres had cost us about an hour and a half in time, which meant that we had extended our journey by some fifteen to twenty miles, using up a corresponding amount of fuel.

I decided that our best plan would be to go on until we had used up most of the fuel, and to keep a small reserve in case we had to avoid shallows or sandbanks or had to make a spurt to reach a ship. But on investigation we found that the fuel tank was securely fastened by a cap which, lacking tools, we were unable to unscrew. Penknives proved useless, however hard we tried. That meant we should just have to go on as long as the fuel lasted.

About seven o'clock that night the engine began to cough and shortly after gave out altogether. We had no very accurate knowledge of our position, but I reckoned we were within twenty miles of the British coast. We peered hard towards the west; a night adrift was no pleasant prospect. But all we could see was the grey horizon and a few cotton-wool clouds. Suddenly all three of us exclaimed and pointed at a strip of coast with lighthouse, trees, ships—it was nothing but a mirage that dissolved within seconds.

The weather, which up till then had been perfect, was now beginning to freshen. Moreover, we were caught in a current that was carrying us the wrong way—in a southeasterly direction. There was no point in rowing. With two inexperienced men, in a heavy launch, it would have been a wasted effort. It seemed better to save our strength until there was something worth rowing to. We saw a wreck, which was not encouraging, as it indicated that we were in shallow waters, which again meant a risk of running on to a sandbank or being caught in the surf. And as darkness fell the wind grew stronger. We had to get out the oars, and I saw to it that my companions went to work the right way to keep the launch under control. Before long we were all three soaked with spray. I thought of my original attempt to cross in a canoe: if we had succeeded in getting away we should very soon have gone down in a choppy sea.

Through the night we fought on. It was clear that we were not far from shore, and at intervals we could see searchlights in the west. Our main fear was that we might be held by a current that would carry us into the Channel. We had heard stories of people trying to escape who had been washed ashore in occupied France. De Korver and Den Ouden were beginning to suffer from seasickness and were becoming less and less capable of manning the oars. I had to shout at them, if only to keep them awake and conscious. I could not keep the launch head-on to the waves with the rudder alone.

[35]

Towards morning the wind dropped and I sighed with relief, for now I could manage alone again. I surveyed the scene. The sea was grey, endlessly grey. My two companions had fallen asleep where they were, lost to the world. I myself could hardly keep awake, but I had to force myself to remain watchful, for I alone knew how to handle the launch. The sky of the new day was grey and sunless, but fortunately the wind had changed and we were now being propelled in a south-westerly direction.

Planes passed overhead, and we tried to attract their attention by waving garments, but in vain. Our morale was beginning to flag badly. The day crept on, and midday brought a glimmer of sunshine. We sat slumped in our seats. We had no cigarettes left and were running short of drinking water. Our lips were beginning to tingle. We hardly spoke.

Evening came, bringing no change. We had ceased to think of ourselves as conquering heroes. We thought of home instead. The wind had dropped altogether, and I had discovered that we were right on top of a sandbank with not much more than six or seven feet of water under our keel, which was another setback, as it meant that we could expect no ships in the vicinity.

Night fell. Our bodies were beginning to feel sore, our eyes ached with staring. But I had lost the wish to sleep. I was somnolently awake, my head feeling light and my ears ringing. A large blackness loomed up ahead—a kind of buoy. I put my companions to work again and we rowed towards it, to find that it was a Red Cross buoy for saving airmen. These buoys would take four people and were supposed to be visited at regular intervals by the Air-Sea Rescue. Well, we were at any rate getting near civilization.

In the early morning we ran aground on a sandbank, and, looking ahead, I could see some beacons which meant we were in an offshore channel. I woke the other two and told them that here was our great chance and something to do. At that moment we saw the barrage balloons of a convoy in the distance. All our tiredness fell from us. We jumped overboard on to the sandbank in barely two feet of water and dragged the launch across the sands with our united strength. The bulk of the convoy passed without noticing us though we waved like madmen. I fired my pistol into the air, but even that passed unobserved. The distance was too great. At last a trawler, out on one side of the convoy, spotted us and began to blow her siren. It was clearly signalling to us, though we had no idea what message she was trying to convey. We rowed towards her for all we were worth and as we drew nearer saw that she was a naval vessel, H.M. minesweeper *Wardour*.

The nearer we got the greater was the shouting that went on. Everyone was gesturing and pointing and we wondered what it was all about. They threw down a rope-ladder and a line and we climbed on board, while a British sailor made arrangements to take our launch in tow. I left the launch last as befitted my role of leader, and I stepped on deck just in time to see Den Ouden throwing his arms round the captain's neck. The captain grinned a bit, patted Den Ouden's shoulder and gave him a cigarette. Then he began a complicated speech, little of which I understood, but enough to gather that we had rowed straight through a minefield. We were some fifteen miles east of Sheerness, so that we were off the Thames estuary, or about eighty miles south of our proposed course.

We were conducted to the crew's quarters, and everyone on board did all he could to make us welcome. Chocolate was produced and Player's cigarettes, and we were plied with navy rum and, to top it all, with a good meal of pork and beans. Not that we were able to eat much. As soon as we took our first mouthfuls the reaction set in. I woke to find my bearded face resting on the table and was told we were about to enter Sheerness. We saw the lighthouse, the green coastline, houses, ships. Not a mirage, this time.

CHAPTER 4

THE PATRIOTIC SCHOOL

A COUPLE of British soldiers in khaki uniforms were waiting on the quay for us; they wore funny red caps and white belts. A band round their right arms bore the letters M.P. That must mean Military Police. One of them had the most enormous moustache I had ever seen, but when he spoke we found it wasn't to hide a harelip, for his words sounded quite natural for English. He gave us what must have been a regulation salute, solemnly welcomed us to a free country, and, with a thousand excuses, relieved me of my pistol, which he handled as if it were a toy.

We were escorted to a waiting car and were constantly offered cigarettes. The one without a moustache kept on slapping his thigh and exclaiming, "Jesus Christ, and in an open launch!"

We were told that we were on our way to Chatham, to the police station—no, no, only a formality. "Well, this is one way of sailing up the Medway," I thought.

At the police station we were searched and then given tea. We were placed side by side on chairs, facing a courteous police officer, who plied us with questions. In the absence of an interpreter the interrogation became a little fantastic, but throughout it remained business-like and cautious. At the end of it, our possessions were returned to us, though certain articles were placed in large envelopes and solemnly sealed.

After this first interrogation we were taken to London. It was a fine day and, in spite of the many uniforms to be seen, life seemed to us to be going on fairly normally. We did see some ruined buildings, but there was nothing particularly eerie about them. Men in dungarees were working on them, and people walked past the bombed sites, reading newspapers and taking little notice of them. So this was the panic-stricken London about which we had read "reports from neutral sources" in the German-controlled Dutch press. It was obviously a city that had stripped off its finery, but people looked neither depressed nor defeated. On the contrary. They all looked supremely confident and fearless—a fact that impressed us most of all, coming as we did from occupied territory.

Our first port of call was the Patriotic School in a London suburb, a central point where all arrivals from occupied Europe were screened for reliability—a logical arrangement of which we sincerely approved, for it was obvious that the Germans must have tried to send their agents to England by the "innocent" route that we had followed. In the course of our stay at the Patriotic School I had the pleasure of seeing a Frenchman caught out; he was carrying a microphotograph of a radio code hidden in his wristwatch.

We were well treated and every hour saw our strength recuperating. Many things were pleasurably exciting: we could openly listen to Radio Orange, we could read newspapers freely—newspapers that were so obviously not filled with lies. A heavy weight had fallen from our shoulders.

On the fourth day we were given a clean bill of health and handed over to the Dutch authorities. We were asked by the Dutch to report on conditions in the homeland.

I was the first member of the *Jan van Galen* crew to have come over, and I was amazed at how little the people over here knew of conditions in occupied territory or of the May days and the sinking of the *Jan van Galen*.

I was particularly delighted with the news that my brother had come over safely and was serving in the depot-ship *Stuijvesant* at Holyhead.

A day or so later we were received in audience by Her Majesty Queen Wilhelmina, a privilege accorded to all who succeeded in making their way across. We felt exceedingly awkward and clumsy in the drawing-room of her modest country house on the outskirts of London. But the Queen received us with warm friendliness and we were struck by the informality of her conversation. Would we come for a walk in her garden and tell her all about the journey across? Only two weeks before, we had been in hiding, running the risk of arrest at any moment by some German rustic in uniform, and here we were, in an English garden, walking along between syringa bushes, talking to a friendly grey-haired lady, a Queen.

The following day we were taken to see Prince Bernhard, who was very jovial and asked us what our plans were: which branch of the services we were hoping to join. I was keen on getting into the air force, but my ignorance of English put that out of the question for the time being. The Prince advised me to set to, put my back into it, and come and see him again when I thought my English had sufficiently improved. Meanwhile, I had better join the crew of the *Isaac Sweers*, as there was a shortage of experienced naval personnel. But before I did that, would I care to spend a week or two on board the *Stuijvesant* in the company of my brother and get the hang of things over here?

[41]

I reported at the Naval H.Q. and was given a kitbag and a completely new outfit. For the first time in many months I felt myself again. With De Korver, who had been made a naval barber, first class, I set off to Holyhead. I took leave of Den Ouden, who was to be a gunner in the Dutch Fleet Air Arm. It was the last time I saw him; he was killed over Norway shortly afterwards.

I was very moved when I came face to face with my brother on board the Dutch warship. It was a moment to which I had been looking forward for more than a year. We had a lot to tell each other. As we sat in a smoky harbour pub over a drink, it was just like being in Flushing in the old days. My brother grinned. "I knew you wouldn't stick it under the Germans. But you took your time coming over, didn't you?"

It didn't take me long to get used to life on board ship again. If anything, I was bored, and longed for action. I was glad to be transferred towards the end of August to the *Isaac Sweers*, which was stationed at Greenock on the west coast of Scotland. It took me twelve hours to get there. The captain told me I was to be chief gunner; that is to say, I was to be in charge of sighting and firing the whole battery. That would be nothing new to me, for I had done the same work on board the lost *Jan van Galen*. I knew dozens of the men on board, and I felt truly at home. We sailed that first evening.

The sun withdrew behind the bare mountain slopes and a dark and woolly mist rose from the clefts of the broad, fjord-like estuary. In the dull silver waters of the Clyde were gathered a complete fleet of the most heterogeneous craft. Rarely had I seen so many ships together —it was staggering. There was a convoy consisting of a large number of troopships, tankers and transports, with an escort of two aircraft-carriers, two battleships, several heavy cruisers and a cordon of some thirty destroyers, the fleet's greyhounds, whose main task was to find enemy submarines and destroy them with depth-charges.

Night fell rapidly. The signal to leave was given, and on all sides we could hear the bosuns' pipes and a hoarse hooting that reverberated from the hills to die away over the waters. Gradually stillness descended on the scene until all that could be heard was the regular beat of engines, the rush of water against the bows and the swirl round the propellers. The convoy was utterly blacked out and slid into the pitch-blackness of the night. The utmost care was taken by all, for one foolish action, one gleam of light flashing across the sea, might endanger the lives of thousands.

I could not help remembering the stories of German espionage that I had been told at the Patriotic School. Seeing the size of that convoy, it was brought home to me what one brief signal by a German agent to an enemy submarine could bring about. In my imagination I heard the dull thud of explosions, I saw the helpless soldiers and sailors rushing to the sides of burning, unmanageable ships, diving into the water to certain death.

We were well off shore by this time; it was beginning to rain and the wind was rising. I stood by the rail in my oilskins, in a world of my own: the rest had been reduced to vague phantoms. A new but pleasing monotony set in: days and nights of watches, sharp look-outs, meals, and exhausted dreamless sleep in a hammock until the next watch. It was a regularity that kept the nerves taut and from which there would be no relaxation until harbour was reached. Even during those last weeks of summer the North Atlantic was not a pleasant place, especially in a warship. The constant spray and the rain turned the

[43]

watches into a dog's life. The crew were divided into two watches, each with six hours on and six hours off: an invariable routine unless something special had to be done—unless there was an alert, for instance—for then all hands had to be available, sleep or no sleep, watch or no watch, food or no food.

The crew of the *Isaac Sweers* was made up of some hundred and eighty men, a most curious assortment. The cadre mainly consisted of professional navy people, but the rest . . . ! There were young fishermen from Ymuiden and Scheveningen, men from Canada and South America, all Dutch subjects but often unable to speak or understand a word of Dutch. Yet so eager had they been to help defend the fatherland of their parents that they had volunteered from half across the world.

I soon found how different life had become on board ship compared with pre-war days. Certain navigational aspects, of course, remained constant, but the element of play, of make-believe, had gone, and an entirely new spirit animated the men, from the captain to the youngest sailor. There was complete unanimity, for we all knew that the slightest dereliction of duty could have the gravest results and was no longer merely a matter of disciplinary action. And yet the *Isaac Sweers* would not have been a Dutch ship, would not have been distinguishable from any British ship, had not every single member of the crew groused without ceasing. For no Dutch sailor is happy unless he is grousing at anything and everything. The food was largely tinned food, and rich. It kept every grouser at an everlastingly high pitch of grousing satisfaction. And do not imagine that the captain himself was exempt from this national characteristic. I sometimes thought that he outdid the rest. We were perfectly happy.

Not that the *Isaac Sweers* was the only ship from

foreign parts in the convoy. There were several Australian ships, and even a Polish vessel. It was remarkable to see all acting in concert in this well-integrated unit and reacting with lightning speed to every order from the nerve centre like the limbs of a healthy body. Externally, the nationalities of the ships could be told by their flags, but once on board the differences were even more striking. On each of those few thousand square feet of ship national life was carried on with religious intensity. While the British had rum and the Poles vodka, we had Dutch gin. In action we all seemed to behave in much the same way, at least where submarines and aircraft were concerned. But face to face with the enemy, reactions varied greatly: for instance, in the attitude towards prisoners of war. If German airmen were rescued and taken on board, the British would treat them courteously, give them a cigarette and a cup of tea—behaviour emotionally foreign to the Dutch, who would clap them behind lock and bar as fast as they could. To Australians, prisoners of war meant literally nothing, they barely noticed them; the Poles, in contrast, having suffered most at German hands, were probably the fiercest among us, as the following incident, which occurred on one of the convoy trips, will show.

A Polish destroyer had forced a German submarine to the surface by some well-placed depth-charges, and some twenty members of the German crew were picked up. The Polish captain made them all stand to attention in a row on deck and then gave the order, "Forward, march!" The Germans took five steps forward and came to the edge of the deck. There German discipline faltered. Again the Polish captain shouted, "Forward, march!" And the Germans marched over the edge to their deaths. Upon arrival at the next Allied port, military police stood ready to receive the prisoners of war.

"We have no prisoners," the captain assured them. That Polish captain was most surprised at the British insistence, and even more surprised when he was sentenced to a term in gaol.

After a few days in the stormy Atlantic the convoy began to follow a more southerly course and the weather improved. The Dutch could no longer grouse about the rain and the cold, but they had the blinding sun, which turned the decks into blistering ovens, to keep them up to the mark. There were a few alarms during the voyage. Depth-charges were dropped without scoring a hit, but at the same time the entire convoy was kept intact. After about a fortnight we were somewhere north of the Azores and were relieved by a Mediterranean escort. The Atlantic escort returned to Scotland to repeat its performance.

Our first encounter with aeroplanes occurred in the Irish Sea, when Stukas were dive-bombing a convoy in the vicinity. We beat off the German planes with no material losses or casualties.

After having completed another convoy trip, the *Isaac Sweers* entered the harbour of Londonderry in the north to take in oil, and then went on to Southampton for repairs. There we were given a few days' shore leave and I was made an ordnance corporal.

At Southampton our camouflage was changed. We were given the light-brown colour common to ships in tropical waters. And although nothing was said, it was clear that our next trip would mean goodbye to Old England for some time.

During our last night in Southampton there was a heavy bombing raid. I was in town that night and had a chance to see the English under bombardment. The attack was fierce, but nothing compared with the fighting spirit of the people. Fires were springing up everywhere, a small-scale replica of what I had seen in Rotterdam. But the personnel of the National Fire Service carried on their fire-fighting activities as if there was no such thing as a rain of bombs. With British phlegm they wasted not an instant but tackled every fire as it broke out. I saw them entering raging infernos in their attempts to save lives; it was obvious that the number of casualties was going to be high, but I saw no trace of panic. It was all remarkably well organized, and those amateur firemen who had probably spent most of their lives in dusty offices, or in making doorknobs in some factory, behaved as if they had been trained to their highly dangerous work from infancy.

The next morning, as I stood surveying the smouldering ruins of an entire district, I saw shopkeepers organizing open-air sales, knocking together stalls and putting them up amidst the rubble with notices such as: "Business as usual. Today's special bargains! Shop-soiled goods at greatly reduced prices", "Please wipe your feet before entering!" or "Who is this Adolf Hitler?"

Back on board, I was told the story of two Dutch sailors who had been caught in the air-raid. They had been actively celebrating their shore leave and were in the merriest of moods when the sirens went. When the worst was over they heard that a nearby shelter had been blocked by a fall of rubble in the middle of which lay an unexploded time-bomb. Full of strong drink and fellow-feeling, the two Dutchmen made for the rubble, routed round and dragged out the time-bomb. Then they staggered around until they met someone who lent them the screwdriver they were asking for, and back to the bomb they went, unscrewed the time-fuse and threw it away, and then set off in search of some more drink. They were horrified the next morning when they learned what their Dutch courage had led them to do. Why, it might have been dangerous, one of them declared, and both wisely nodded their heads. No one was more surprised than they to hear that they had been sent medals for bravery by the King.

CHAPTER 5

SAILORS DON'T WORRY

REPAIRS to the *Isaac Sweers* were soon finished, and we left in haste for Greenock to pick up a convoy. The first part of the trip went as usual, but this time we sailed past the Azores to enter the harbour of Freetown on the African west coast, some two or three weeks later. The heat out there was murderous. The white city lay shimmering in the tropical sun, and the beer and fruit hawked by pedlars with baskets and crates looked very inviting—equally inviting were the beauties that strolled on the quays with their eye on the ship. But we had to savour these delights from afar—from the glowing plates of the deck, in short. We took in oil and left the same day, sailing northward in the company of an Australian destroyer, our destination Gibraltar.

Though the English had been cheerful enough, England's sombre climate with its depressing autumn mists made Gibraltar, in contrast, an El Dorado. There the weather was lovely, and, compared with many other ports, prices were dirt cheap. Only for those who hankered after female company was it a disappointment. For there were no women. At least there were plenty of the genuine Spanish types dancing in the various cafés and cabarets and giving us a flurry of skirts to admire, but come eleven o'clock of a night and they all left the garrison town under military escort. Whisky and sweet wines, which were both plentiful, helped us to forget our lack of female company, and the cafés were idyllic places, for even if the guitar music did come from radiograms the illusion was there.

Why we were being kept at Gibraltar was an impenetrable mystery to us, but sailors don't worry. We'd know soon enough, we reckoned, and made what we could of the fleeting days. The solution came before very long when the entire crew was mustered and a high-ranking British officer came on board: Admiral Somerville, in command of the fleet in the Western Mediterranean. He was a genial man about whom many flattering stories went the rounds. We often heard it said, "Wish there were more like him."

The admiral looked us Dutch sailors up and down, and by the smile on his face we judged that he liked what he saw. He liked the Dutch, he told us. They were fine sailors. And he added that our ancestors had often been after his—too often, in fact. But now we had a chance of being after the same game together. From this moment our ship was under his supreme command. And he did not wish to hide the facts of the case: there was a bad time ahead. We must do convoy work to Malta and back, for that island must be kept at all costs. If Malta fell into the hands of the enemy the Allies would lose their hold over the Mediterranean. In any case there was extensive patrolling to be done to prevent the German submarines getting through the Straits of Gibraltar. Somerville went on to tell us that he had joined the British navy as a thirteen-year-old lad and that now he was sixty-one he had risen to be an admiral. But the older the fiddle, the sweeter the tune. He intended to prove that, and now we had met we'd know each other in future and would know better where we stood. So what about it?

[50]

We gave "the old seahorse" (for that was the nickname by which we knew him) three rousing cheers. He had certainly given us confidence, for we knew he liked us. We had already had evidence of that. On the last day of August, which was our Queen's birthday, there had been two or three Dutch submarines at Gibraltar, and the Dutch had decided to celebrate the occasion. Now there is a custom in Gibraltar that on closing the cafés at night "God Save the King" is played and everyone stands to attention. On this special occasion the band had been asked to play our national anthem as well; when it did, the British present took no notice and pointedly sat down. The Dutch took offence and words soon turned to blows. The Dutch, though in a minority, were so furious that the café was wrecked and ambulances had to collect the casualties. Somerville, on hearing of this episode, was livid with fury—not with the Dutch but with his own countrymen.

"What if they were all drunk? Of course they were. But drunk or sober, they will respect their Dutch allies." And he issued an order of the day giving us a pat on the back and his own men a severe reprimand.

Before long the *Isaac Sweers* was sailing the blue sea with a convoy of a dozen ships, escorted by battleships, cruisers, destroyers and aircraft-carriers, which last included the *Ark Royal*, an enormous floating aerodrome carrying some seventy planes and a crew of eighteen hundred.

Though the sub-tropical climate of the Mediterranean was far pleasanter than anything we had had so far, especially compared with the treacherous Atlantic at this season, we soon found that its warfare was considerably more intensive—a disadvantage that outweighed the pleasures of the climate. For the Allies were only just able to maintain themselves against the modern Italian fleet, supported as it was by a very powerful air arm. The Italians had safe air bases within reach, and what they lacked in sea-power they could at any moment supplement from the air. The moment the battle became too hot they could retire to their conveniently situated bases.

Our convoy was halfway between Gibraltar and Sardinia when an Italian long-range reconnaissance plane began to shadow it. It was soon shot down by a fighter plane from the *Ark Royal*, but evidently not before the pilot had reported details to his base. Two hours later, when I had just gone below at the end of my watch and was sitting down in readiness for my meal, the alarm klaxon sounded. We put down our knives and forks on the plates that had just been filled with steaming food and hurried up on deck, strapping on our helmets as we went. The men who were sleeping in the hammocks rolled out and staggered a few steps before fully realizing what it was all about; in any case, we slept fully dressed even to life-jackets. Everyone was cursing those damned chimney-sweeps, as we called the Italians, those rats who wouldn't leave us a moment's peace. Within two minutes we were all at action stations, surreptitiously fastening our shoelaces.

A swarm of Italian torpedo-bombers came over, already being fired at by the ships on the other side of the large convoy we were escorting. This was my first experience of an engagement of any magnitude, and I stood trembling in my shoes with subdued emotion. Rotterdam had been nothing to this.

The Italians came on with infuriating confidence, often within thirty feet of the water. The radiant sky of unbroken blue became rapidly flecked with the bursts of anti-aircraft shells. All the ships were firing by now, and the acrid smoke of gunpowder was hanging like a mist over the sea. British fighters were swooping on the enemy planes like birds of prey. All the planes were firing, and battery upon battery of 5-inch guns was thundering a reply to the Italian fire; through it rang the vicious yapping of the ack-ack guns and the shrill rattle of machineguns. And above the uproar the steady drone and whine of aircraft.

The battleship *Nelson* was struck by a torpedo near the bow, but although she began to lose speed she ploughed on with determination. I saw her carrying on a method of fighting which, even though the situation was serious, made me burst out laughing. As the Italians were coming in so low, the *Nelson* could not use her mighty 16-inch guns in the normal way, but her crew were aiming at the sea so that enormous columns of water spouted up and hit the planes fair and square. It was a brilliant display of gunnery that was inspiring even if faintly comic.

The first wave of the attack was over in about fifteen minutes. The men tipped their helmets back over their necks and wiped their heated foreheads. Fine, we were still alive. Gradually we were able to survey results within sight: twelve Italians shot down to three of our Fulmars and some damage to the *Nelson*. How serious this damage was we could not tell, but she was steaming on and did not seem to be settling. I saw her in dock a few days later with a hole in her side in which one could have turned round a horse and cart.

It was not to be expected that the Italians would leave it at that. We used the momentary lull to slip away to the mess-deck to finish our interrupted meal; but, alas, in order to dodge torpedoes the ship had been turning hairpin bends and the food and crockery were all over the deck, a sticky mass of food and broken china. One of the men slipped on it and fell; when he regained his feet he looked like something out of a slapstick comic film. The joke was on us, for there wasn't a thing left fit to eat. Later we were to learn that the chimney-sweeps always attacked at mealtimes, whatever time meals were: a coincidence, no doubt, but it made us feel particularly bitter, having to man the batteries on empty stomachs, thinking of the nice warm food that was being hurled about the mess-deck.

About an hour after the first affray the klaxons went again, and again our stomachs gave that curious heave. This time there were some twenty-five Italian torpedo-bombers, but the British fighters got off the mark earlier and intercepted more than half of the attackers. And again no great damage was done. But at the same time our reconnaissance planes reported the presence of a strong Italian naval squadron steaming full speed ahead about twenty-five miles distant from our convoy. This was a temptation "the old seahorse" could not resist. The order to attack was given forthwith. We would be in a minority, of course, for we could not withdraw all the warships from the convoy.

The *Sweers* was among the lucky ones chosen for attack. Flying a large Dutch flag, we briskly changed course, and it was soon apparent that the *Isaac Sweers* was the fastest destroyer afloat in the Mediterranean. While the British ships were going full out, we were using only about eighty-five per cent of our engine force and still had four or five knots in hand. But fast as we were, the Italians were faster. As soon as they realized what was happening they sheered off, and there was no chance of catching them up within a reasonable distance.

With all this going on, we had meanwhile succeeded in bringing our convoy to the Straits of Sicily, probably the most dangerous point of the whole route. As soon as darkness fell, the convoy, accompanied by only a few destroyers, went on alone because of the danger of mines. The *Sweers* turned through a hundred and eighty degrees and made for Gibraltar. Less than an hour later we saw a red glow in the sky. One of the transports had hit a mine and was ablaze. The next day we heard that the entire convoy, with this one exception, had arrived safely at Malta.

During the weeks that followed we repeatedly covered this same route, but we never passed through the Straits of Sicily, for they were absolutely sealed off by mines. As the convoys to Malta had mainly been carrying crates with fighter planes for the island, we now used a safer if more laborious method. The fighters, with their relatively small operational range, would be assembled at Gibraltar and placed on two or three aircraft-carriers that sailed as far as the entrance to the Straits of Sicily. There the fighters would take off to join battle against the swarms of Stukas and similar aircraft that were trying to reduce the heroic British stronghold of Malta.

On our return from one of these trips, with the Rock of Gibraltar already in sight, the *Ark Royal* was hit by two torpedoes from a German submarine that had obviously been lying in wait in some Spanish inlet. It was about five in the afternoon, and before long the aircraft-carrier was seen to be developing a marked list. The aeroplanes on her deck were sliding, slowly but surely, towards the edge of the deck and the sea below. The crew were being taken off except for those who remained to work the pumps, and a few destroyers stood by to discourage possible enemy submarines with depth-charges. We were one of the destroyers. Throughout the night the *Ark Royal* remained afloat, but by the morning the pumps could no longer compete with the sea, and the end was swift. Only one life was lost.

It was a sad experience to see this proud ship go down within sight of harbour. We of the *Sweers* stood by, powerless to help save the vessel that was famous for her feats earlier in the war during the Norwegian affray. We heard it said that the ship could easily have been saved if the captain, a diehard traditionalist, had not refused to be taken in tow and had not attempted to make harbour under his own steam. Even the assistance of the *Theems*, a powerful Dutch tug that was standing by throughout, was refused. It would indeed have been a grand manœuvre if the *Ark Royal* could have saved herself—a great honour for the crew, the captain and the navy. But —the ship sank.

This incident stressed once again the ambiguous nature of Spanish neutrality. Fascist Spain was clearly allowing her supposedly neutral territorial waters to be used by her German comrades, who could make good use of the cover provided by the dozens of natural harbours and rocky inlets along the coast. Spain was a hotbed of spies, who were given every facility to watch the Straits of Gibraltar. With my own eyes I have seen lights flashing signals from Spanish soil when one of our convoys set out.

On the Atlantic side the German submarines were like hornets, trying to edge their way into the Mediterranean. I was told of a remarkable duel between a German and a Dutch submarine. The Dutch had five submarines stationed at Gibraltar and they were the terror of the comic Italian fleet. One night, as one of the Dutch submarines surfaced she saw within a short distance a German submarine which had—as had the Dutch—considered the time and place convenient for replenishing the batteries needed for under-water navigation. The Germans also noticed their neighbour, and for a few moments the two craft eyed each other like vicious sharks. And the German must have failed to observe that his opponent was a Dutch submarine and not a British one—an important distinction because not all the British submarines were equipped to fire torpedoes from the stern, whereas all the Dutch were. So the Germans, convinced that they could hit their opponent before she could get ready to fire, attempted a rapid manœuvre, thereby presenting a fine target to the Dutch submarine, which, without moving, discharged a torpedo from the stern. A satisfactory moment. In triumph, twenty prisoners of war were taken to Gibraltar, and days later the German commander was still cursing the "verfluchte Holländer". It was a sore blow to his pride that he, the great German, had been neatly caught by a negligible Dutchman.

CHAPTER 6

THE HIGH SEAS

DURING the second week of December 1942 the *Isaac Sweers* was given orders to proceed, together with the British destroyers *Legion* and *Sikh* and their Australian colleague *Maori*, through the Straits of Sicily past Malta to join the Allied fleet in the Eastern Mediterranean. That fleet, under the command of Admiral Cunningham, was in need of reinforcements.

R.A.F. fighters had observed a channel through the minefields, and on December 10th the four ships set out. We realized that it was a perilous undertaking, but we had the fullest confidence in our leaders. We had learnt to know the British and their superbly competent seamanship and the brilliant daring of their exploits. The day before we were due to enter the Straits of Sicily we were being shadowed by an Italian reconnaissance plane, which assured us that there would be a warm welcome awaiting us. Everything seemed to be going well. Night came, and the four of us were gliding along in line through the tepid darkness. We were scared of mines, of course, for there was so little one could do about the wretched things. About one o'clock the klaxons went as we were off Cape Bon. The *Legion*, our leader, had detected the enemy. We reduced speed to about five knots in order not to show bow-wave or wake and crept close in to the coast to hide our outlines against the rocky Tunisian shore. Slowly and carefully we slid between the enemy squadron and the coast; the Italians were not more than two miles off shore. Fortunately there was no moon.

The enemy appeared to consist of two cruisers and a number of destroyers and M.T.B.s. Although tension was rapidly becoming unbearable, we knew that here was an enemy we could tackle if need be.

The Italians were blissfully unaware of our presence; they must have been keeping a look-out seaward. When the *Legion* and the others had the enemy at about ninety degrees on the port side the leader fired all her torpedoes at the first cruiser. The surprise was as complete as the effect. The night seemed to explode. In one second the cruiser was a mass of flames. The other cruiser had meanwhile been tackled by the *Sikh* and the *Maori*. The *Sweers* had also opened fire on the second cruiser and then on a heavy destroyer that came steaming along with the obvious intention of ramming her. The *Sweers* just managed to avoid the onslaught and to disable the attacker. Distances were so small—all within two hundred yards—that it was hardly possible to miss one's target. I could plainly see the Italians in their white uniforms dashing about the decks, and I could see the gleam of glass and steel as our shells exploded and flames leapt out of the destroyer.

The whole encounter lasted perhaps ten minutes. We had got rid of them, a startling victory. Because of our scrap with the destroyer we had fallen a little astern, and the British ships turned right round to have a look for us and render any assistance that might be needed. We, however, were in the pink, not a scratch on our paintwork —nor had the other three sustained any damage. Enemy losses amounted to two cruisers, one M.T.B. and a destroyer on fire, due entirely to the cool and daring tactics of the *Legion*.

I had gradually become used to dearly-bought victories and it was unbelievable that on this occasion we had inflicted a serious defeat on the enemy without suffering a single casualty ourselves—no one dead, no one wounded, in spite of the fact that the enemy had sent tracer bullets ricochetting all over our decks. And I have not mentioned that the coastal batteries of the Pétain-French had also opened fire on us. Those gentry were not recognized by us, and by the Axis powers only when it suited them, which, judging by their marksmanship, was only according to their deserts.

The four of us made straight for Malta in an effort to be within escort range by daybreak, for if we were not we were in for a tough time, as the Italians were by this time probably beside themselves with rage. And at ten o'clock in the morning we safely entered the harbour of Valetta, where we were given a delirious reception. The news of our victory had gone ahead by radio and thousands of the inhabitants stood waving and cheering. The warships in the harbour were dressed over all, their crews standing to attention lining the rails. The band of the flagship struck up first "God Save the King" and then the "Wilhelmus", the Dutch national anthem. We thrust out our chests—proud as peacocks.

From all the houses that still stood in that battered little town flags were flying, and everywhere we went we were stood free drinks. The spontaneous friendliness of these people who, for years now, had been subjected to the most gruelling bombardments was touching. There they were, laughing and joking among the ruins, those Maltese, and they could be sure that within a few days they would be having another battering and more names would be added to the lengthy list of casualties.

To return to our naval engagement in the Straits of

Sicily: with typical German insolence the German H.Q. announced that day—an announcement preceded by the usual blare of trumpets—that the Dutch destroyer the *Isaac Sweers* had been sunk in the Mediterranean. Our crew did not know whether to be angry, indignant or amused. Immediately the news was out Admiral Cunningham arranged for a large wreath to be delivered on board our ship with a card which bore the words: "Many happy returns from the bottom of the sea!"

But the war went on. Admittedly we had reminded our allies of our existence, but as soon as we had left Valetta there were other things to think of than past deeds of valour. We were now escorting a large convoy from Malta going eastward. Our destination was Alexandria, and the trip was remarkably easy. A few air attacks were made—not particularly vicious ones—before our convoy safely reached its goal. That, at any rate, was how it struck us then.

Half an hour after we had tied up the air was suddenly filled with the roar of heavy explosions. The battleships *Valiant* and *Queen Elizabeth* had been hit and had sprung leaks. No one knew what had happened. There was not a plane in sight. Sabotage? Or carelessness? Surely not. The mystery was cleared up by a few depth-charges dropped in the harbour by some small craft. An Italian pocket-submarine had crept into the harbour as the convoy was being passed through the boom and the crew had affixed explosive limpets to the two largest warships —and had waited a few minutes.

Before long the Italian surfaced. With smiling faces the crew allowed themselves to be taken prisoner, very proud of themselves. And in our hearts we could not disagree with them.

Alexandria is an ugly, dishevelled town, with much

open poverty and some very loud amusements. It was the favourite leave centre of the Eighth Army soldiers coming in for a breather in between scraps with Rommel. The atmosphere was objectionable, though understandable. So many men felt that they might as well enjoy themselves today, for they would be dead tomorrow. Active service must have been intolerable in that climate, especially as the German Afrika Korps was still dominant—a situation that did not improve the Eighth Army temper. That was very noticeable. We, too, fought daily duels with death, but we were fighting in a setting that was our own, not in some lousy desert. Who on earth could conjure up any enthusiasm for those inhospitable stretches of sand?

Eighth Army leave meant drink and women, both in the greatest possible quantity and at top speed. Time was short. The Australians were adepts at the fast technique. It was very plain that those tough hunks of men were not strolling about Alexandria to admire any Columns of Pompey or the catacombs. I once watched them, in the bright noonday sun, stop a lorry loaded with crates of beer, chase the frightened Arab driver away, and empty the crates on the spot to the last drop.

To watch life in Alexandria was more depressing than to watch a battle against odds when one's own side was in a decided minority: in that leave centre morality had fallen back to its most primitive crudity. Not that the Dutch didn't have a good time in Alexandria. There were a good many South Africans in town, looking like overgrown Boy Scouts in their shorts and broad-brimmed hats. They were invariably friendly to us, aware perhaps of racial kinship. Whenever we found ourselves involved in a brawl the South Africans would join in and help chastise whoever was bothering us.

We returned to Malta from Alexandria. If the Western Mediterranean had been no picnic, the eastern basin was worse. Not a day passed without air-raids, and these raiders were not Italians but Germans in their deadly Junkers 88, nasty brutes, operating from bases on Crete. We could breathe freely only at night; during the day we were manning the guns from dawn to dusk, without time even to light a cigarette, let alone sleep. Mealtimes were still bound to go awry.

As we drew near Malta dive-bombers were replaced by torpedo-bombers, swooping boldly on the convoy from every angle. It was almost comic at times. Our captain, Lieutenant-Commander Harmsen, was a short man who could hardly see over the rail of the bridge. For that reason he generally stood on a chair that had been nailed to the deck. He always smoked enormous cigars, except at night, and in moments of stress he would chew as much as smoke. The crew had unlimited confidence in him, for he was an excellent sailor and never fussed. It was his habit to allow the torpedo-bombers to come in close, until they were actually dropping their missiles. He would then deliberately estimate their trajectories and bark sharp orders to turn one way or the other. And we would watch the "tin fish" pass us, sometimes within feet of the hull.

Harmsen gained himself a reputation in the Mediterranean fleet, partly on account of his diminutive stature and partly on account of his everlasting cigar. In one bombing raid a Junker screamed down over us, clearly in for a kill. A stick of bombs fell alongside the ship, enormous columns of water spouted up, hiding us from the other ships like a screen. They all thought we'd had it, but a few moments later we were back in the fray, guns firing. The nearest British vessel politely signalled, "All

O.K.?" And Harmsen's immediate reply went back, "No. Cigar wet."

A legend that we had a charmed life grew, not only among our friends but even among our enemies. The Germans did their best to kill it; three times, if not four, their news service announced that we had been sunk. But it must be admitted that the Germans did not limit themselves to Goebbel's wishful sinkings; they did all they could to make them a fact. Time and time again it was evident that our destruction was becoming a matter of prestige to the enemy. Many of the crew were blaming Radio Orange, the organ of the Dutch Government in London, for boasting about the ship's achievements to such an extent that the enemy was driven to action. And the more one thinks about it the more obvious it seems. The propaganda value of stories about our prowess was enormous: news of the *Sweer*'s deeds must have been balm to the wounded pride of the Dutch in occupied territory. But there were moments when a Radio Orange man would have been taking his life in his hands in coming aboard our ship.

Though the Dutch destroyer and her crew were having one miraculous escape after another, the other ships in the convoy were not proving so lucky. What made this worse was that we had come to know so many of the men in other ships. There were days when we forgot to grouse, days that we spent mourning our friends. We would carry out our duties automatically and think of home, so far away and so decidedly out of our reach; it would seem to us that our lives resembled a rabbit caught in the glare of the headlights of a car. The nearer death came, the more we realized our vulnerability in this world of fire and steel. Ships went down and their places were taken

[64]

by others. War was waged with bitter determination.
Convoys sailed with clockwork regularity, Junkers or no
Junkers. The Allied sailors manned their posts.

Early one morning I had just turned in after an
exhausting night when I was woken by a couple of dull
thuds. I leapt out of my hammock and ran on deck.
Our faithful companion of many a trip, the *Gurkha*, had
been hit and she was already listing heavily. Thick
clouds of black smoke were billowing from the stern and
amidships, and in the stillness of morning the smoke did
not disperse. The two torpedoes, probably discharged by
an Italian submarine that had crept in, were too much for
the *Gurkha*. Her oil tanks had been hit, and before very
long the destroyer was ringed round with a layer of belch-
ing flame.

We received instructions to pick up the crew—a
dangerous task, as the submarine was obviously still
lurking in the vicinity. As we closed in another destroyer
raced round dropping depth-charges. There was a heavy
swell and the lowering of the boats was not easy. We
succeeded in getting a line across to the *Gurkha* to fix a
hawser and tow her out of the burning oil. Not until that
was done could we reach her with our boats to take off
the wounded; the others had to jump overboard and swim
to the *Sweers*, where coffee was being brewed in quantity.

The whole rescue took less than an hour. Slowly the
Gurkha sank. For one instant she stood on end and then
slipped down to the depths. To the last moment a British
sailor stood on the bows holding aloft a flag, and not until
the ship sank under him did he leap into the water and
swim over to us, flag and all. He was hauled on board to
rousing cheers.

Of the crew of two hundred and forty-nine we saved
two hundred and forty-two. The other seven had been

c

killed outright when the torpedoes struck. A number of
the survivors had been badly burnt, however, and it was
necessary to get them to hospital as soon as possible. As
there was no possibility of going into action with a double
crew, we made for Tobruk and there landed our friends
of the *Gurkha*.

Tobruk, a former Italian harbour, was close to the
front line and for many weeks had been holding out
against the savage onslaughts of Rommel's troops. The
garrison made on us an impression very different from
that of the Eighth Army on leave. Here they were ruth-
less combat troops with neither time nor inclination for
throwing their weight about, tough men fighting like
lions.

When we arrived they had not seen fresh bread for
more than three weeks. Potatoes had been used up weeks
ago, and their diet consisted of ships' biscuit, butter, jam,
and herrings in tomato sauce. For every meal, every day.
They were moved to tears when we decided to let them
have all the potatoes and bread we had on board. The
Tommies who came to fetch the provisions sank their
teeth into our stale bread as if it had been cake.

"Chips and bread tonight, boys!" they were shouting,
and one after the other insisted on giving us their home
addresses.

"When you're back in England you must come and
see us. You must try my wife's cooking!" Our stock was
very high at Tobruk. The men there treated us like
heroes. But by the time they were having their chips and
bread and butter the *Sweers* was back on the high seas,
trying to overtake the convoy on its way to Malta.

CHAPTER 7

FOR SPECIAL WORK

EARLY February 1942. Nearly two months had gone by since Japan's treacherous attack on Pearl Harbour had spread the war to the Far East. The United States were now in on our side, and on the first day of the New Year twenty-four Allied nations had joined the Atlantic Charter. The balance was not yet even, however. Thousands of miles were being lost in the Pacific, the East Indies were being invaded, and Singapore was in danger. Japan's rising sun was still in the ascendant.

Events in the West were not conducive to optimism, either. The Germans had advanced deep into the Soviet Union, and, though the Red Army had recovered from the first shock and was returning blow for blow, the German might was still unbroken and a new spring offensive was rumoured. In North Africa the front line was moving backwards and forwards, thousands of lives were being lost with apparently little achieved. Libya was the only theatre of war that could be called elastic— except that that term had not been invented in February 1942. The Axis still had the initiative, and night and day the Luftwaffe directed its fierce attacks on Malta, and on the Allied convoys that had to keep it supplied with much-needed materials.

This was the state of affairs when the *Isaac Sweers* was ordered to the Pacific to take part in the war against

Japan. A wave of enthusiasm passed through the crew—
that was the place for them to be fighting, their Far East.
For ever since war had broken out in the Pacific, it had
been their secret longing to be there, fighting the Japs
as part of an integrated Dutch force. They had no illusion
that the task would be easy, but a number of news items—
"Dutch submarines sink Jap transports", "Dutch planes
disable Jap cruiser"—gave them confidence.

Off Ceylon the *Sweers* had engine trouble and had to
be laid up until the end of February. Repairs done, we
went full speed ahead towards the Straits of Sunda, there
to join a large Dutch naval force. But we were no more
than two days on our way before a signal was received
recalling us to Ceylon. We were too late. The Battle of
the Java Sea had been fought and three-quarters of the
Netherlands fleet had been sunk in combat. The news
left us in terribly low spirits. Had our engines not given
us trouble, we, too, no doubt would have been on the sea
bottom by now. Mingled with our anger and depression
was a certain thankfulness that the *Sweers* had once again
escaped destruction, but we had had enough experience
of war to know that luck would have to smile on us many
a time in the future if we were to come out of it all
unscathed.

Shortly after our return to Colombo, there arrived the
few units that had managed to survive, badly damaged
vessels, packed with survivors. It was a heartrending
spectacle; many of the men were wounded, and we heard
first-hand accounts of the way the Japs were behaving.
The armed might of the once proud Netherlands East
Indies was totally broken.

Round a strong British core a new Far East Fleet was
created under the command of our friend Admiral
Somerville. "The old seahorse" was on the warpath

again, which was some consolation. To this fleet were attached the Dutch frigate *Heemskerk* and our ship, the *Isaac Sweers*, and later the Dutch cruiser *Tromp*, together with several Dutch submarines which had made good their escape.

Within a short space of time a fairly strong fleet had been assembled, its task being to prevent a Japanese invasion of India and Ceylon. But the major shortcoming of this fleet was the lack of aircraft, and these could no longer be dispensed with in naval warfare. The results of the shortage were soon evident: the heavy British cruisers *Cornwall* and *Dorsetshire* were sunk by Japanese suicide pilots, and with them a thousand men went down. A few days later a small aircraft-carrier met the same fate. It was becoming a massacre, and tactics would have to be changed if the Far Eastern Fleet were not to be written off altogether. Admiral Somerville issued an order of the day: all forces must withdraw until such time as there should be a sufficient air cover to fight back successfully. The situation was serious, the old seahorse declared, but there was no cause for foolish despair. "We must avoid battle now, but the day will come when you will return, under my command, and then we shall annihilate the enemy as surely as you call me the old seahorse."

Our temporary base was Mombasa in East Africa, where we spent our time carrying out repairs and taking part in naval manœuvres. It was almost a holiday for us, and we needed it. For more than eighteen months we had been in the thick of the fight, on the worst sea-fronts there were. There were few missiles that we had not had thrown at us. But now life on board had a chance of approaching normality again. And, as with long-distance walkers, we experienced the curious phenomenon of fatigue. Now that we were no longer in action our thoughts turned back to England, and beyond to Holland. The end of the war seemed farther away than ever.

There were moments during watches in those strange, humming, tropical nights when I asked myself what was the point of it all. Why hadn't I stayed quietly at home? What good could I do in this unending murder game? And I would close my eyes for a moment and picture my green island of Walcheren where life had been so sweet and where spring would now be on her way. Fortunately, such moments of weakness rarely lasted very long. I remembered also that last train journey, when I was making my escape from that green island of Walcheren; I remembered those columns of German soldiers tramping our Zeeland lanes, and again their overbearing voices ran in my ears. And I knew that I had done well to get away, that this was the right place for me now that the war had apparently reached its nadir. I had the conviction that I was doing my duty.

One morning the crew were mustered. Commander Harmsen ordered Ordnance-Corporal Pieter Dourlein to step forward. Surprised, I obeyed. The Commander read out a royal decree, and the scene ended with the Bronze Cross being pinned on my chest. Everyone stood to attention and I felt very odd. I was the first member of the crew to be decorated.

A few friends and I were invited to the captain's cabin for a drink—good old-fashioned Dutch gin—and the day mellowed. The captain knew our capacity and he knew how to refill glasses. Nor did he forget to fill his own glass, nor to hand round his precious cigars. To the new wearer of the Bronze Cross the world was growing pleasanter with every passing moment. On leaving the captain's cabin I felt I was in need of a nap, and I stretched out abaft the funnel, where I must have slept for hours, oblivious of the fact that we were getting up steam. I had chosen a bad place to lie down, for when I awoke I was covered with the oily filth that poured from the funnel, and I could easily have passed for one of the Mombasa locals. But being laughed at did not worry me; we had just been told that we were on our way home —back to England, that is to say.

The ship had been in need of a thorough overhaul for some time, and the decision to return had been taken at last; we were to be laid up for repairs at Thornycroft's in Southampton.

Our voyage took us round the Cape of Good Hope, and our first port of call was Durban, a splendid, modern town with shops full of commodities. There it was difficult to believe that there was a war on; the streets were crowded with new cars, trams went at full speed, villas were being freshly painted, streets were brilliantly lit, and illuminated advertisements drew attention to various articles. There was no rationing of food or tobacco, and bombardment was known only from the newspapers. It gave one a ghostly feeling.

After two days we continued our voyage, and, rounding the Cape, we met with the textbook storms. The ship pitched and heaved, and we realized rather suddenly that the sea itself could be dangerous. We had left the sea out of reckoning for so long: submarines, torpedoes, mines and bad weather.

Via cool Capetown and broiling Freetown, on we went to Gibraltar. There the ship was visited by a group of young Dutchmen who had escaped by the arduous overland trek from Holland through Belgium, unoccupied France, and Spain. Some of them were very thin and undernourished, some had suffered in concentration camps. Eagerly they asked if we could take them to England? Someone in authority noticed that there were never as many leaving the ship in the evening as had come on board in the morning. A search was made and fifteen disappointed young men were conducted ashore. When we were well out at sea six more appeared of their own accord. The captain breathed fire, but the crew were very surprised. No, they hadn't known they were there. What could the captain do but give them a smoke and ask them what things were like in Holland?

In mid-June 1942 we arrived safely at Southampton after an absence of nine months. The voyage had been uneventful, though we had zigzagged all the way to evade lurking submarines. In relays, we were given three weeks' shore leave. Mine I spent in London with two of my shipmates. But to have a good time in London money was needed, and the trouble was that we could not draw the whole of our pay; part of it was "frozen", which, on paper, might be a fine thing for married men but was an absurdity for bachelors. At the end of a week, by which time our available cash had run out, we went to the Navy H.Q. in London but found them stony-hearted. We had no wish to spend the rest of our leave sucking a match-stick in some dreary hostel, and we decided to be bold and call on Prince Bernhard, who had the reputation of being willing to help.

At three o'clock we arrived at the Prince's office. The Prince was out, and would we call later. Off we went, to spend what was left of our money in the nearest pub. Drinks went faster than the clock, and over them we discussed which of us should be the spokesman. My two friends were unanimous in thinking I was the one for the job, and I had better have another to help oil my tongue.

By the time the Prince was supposed to be back at his office my tongue was very oiled indeed. Yes, I declared, I'd see to it all. Just leave it to me. I pressed the bell and plied the knocker, and was patting my uniform into proper shape when I observed my two shipmates taking to their heels. I was about to follow them when the door opened and retreat was impossible. I was conducted up a staircase which not only went round corners but seemed to be gently undulating as well. The floors, too, appeared to be made of indiarubber. The next moment I was standing in the Prince's office.

Prince Bernhard came over to me with a smile of welcome and shook hands; he remembered me and asked how my English was getting on. I told him my tongue could not quite manage it, but then I discovered that my tongue could not quite manage the words of my own language either. However, I succeeded in overcoming that difficulty and began what must have resembled a fiery Hyde Park oration. Surreptitiously I had taken hold of a corner of the desk to steady myself, for the floor had not quite settled down.

The Prince laughed a good deal. He understood the situation, for he had the advantage of being cold sober. Repeatedly he patted my shoulder.

"I quite understand," he assured me over and over again. "I entirely agree with you. Yes, of course, it's your money. I'll see what I can do about it." And I was shown out, with another friendly pat on the back.

I could have burst into song as I made my way down the stairs. I very nearly did. As I left the house I saw my two friends peering sheepishly round the nearest corner, and their relief was great when they heard me

call out, "It's all arranged. The Prince is looking into it."
Back to the pub we went, and found that if we pooled all
our money there was enough for one drink each.

The next day we had a message to say that it had been
decided that single men could in future draw a larger
proportion of their pay. That decision put a tidy sum in
our pockets, which we put to good use. After all, what
was the point of saving in war-time?

Three weeks' leave did not alter the fact that our
celebrations constituted only a short break, and as the
end of the three weeks drew near I found myself wondering what was coming next. I was beginning to feel less
keen on going back to sea. Not that I was afraid of the
dangers of a sea life, but I was not looking forward to the
endless monotony of convoy work. I should have preferred a little variation, something that would allow me to
use my own initiative, something that would give me the
feeling that I alone could do that particular job: flying,
for instance. I recollected what Prince Bernhard had told
me during that first interview I had had with him. I had
followed his advice and had learned a good bit of English.
I would ask him for another interview.

The Prince, once again, proved most helpful. He
thought, however, that the moment was not quite propi-
tious for me to go into the air force. But there might be
something else I could do. He told me that people
were needed for special work. Young Dutchmen were
sent back to Holland to gather information about the
Germans and their plans and to make their lives un-
pleasant. It was very dangerous, and if they were caught
by the Nazis the best they could expect was a bullet. If
I wanted to take part in this work, he would find out
whether it could be arranged. He told me to think it
over and to let him know.

There was not much to think about. In Holland I had already discovered how many people there were who were ready to do as much damage as possible to the Germans. But they lacked direction and their efforts suffered from a lack of organization. Many people had discovered that underground work is no business for amateurs. They were caught, and their end usually came one early morning before a German execution squad. While I was still in Holland we had often spoken about the enormous possibilities if this potential army of patriots could only be instructed and led by experienced people from England. There were thousands of young Dutchmen who wanted to join the Allied forces but who found, as I had done, that it was almost impossible to leave the country. No, there was not much to think about. I immediately told Prince Bernhard that I should be glad to be chosen for this special work. I applied to various bodies, and was one day taken to see Lieftinck, Captain of the Marines, and by him to Colonel de Bruyne, head of the Dutch Intelligence Service. So it came about that I was sent to the London School of Military Intelligence.

Later I have often thought about the weeks I spent in London going from one Dutch bureau to another. Things which had seemed normal then took on a rather sinister aspect when my mission to Holland ended in capture by the Nazis before it really had begun. There was too much talk about secret work and there were too many people who seemed to know all about it. One young Dutchman who had taken a few agents to Holland by boat and rowed them ashore at Scheveningen near The Hague had given up in despair when a respectable member of the Dutch Club in London, meeting him one morning in the street, said to him, "I hear you are off to Holland tonight." In the reading-room of the Dutch Club he found a very secret report about the work of the intelligence services and his own part in it. He was not surprised that on his last trip one of the boats had been sunk by the Germans.

A porter at one of the offices I visited told me that his organization dealt with two kinds of people: security-risks (that is, people who might be German spies) and future agents. Both groups met in the waiting-room and often talked in a brotherly way about the horrible experiences they had gone through when coming to England.

"However," the man said, "the future agents are rather easy to recognize. They don't play in the black market or go in for the other kinds of objectionable business which flourish."

At that moment I thought this was not a bad joke. Later it seemed less funny.

CHAPTER 8

A NEW LIFE

COLONEL DE BRUYNE'S offices were in a modern flat in Park Street, and I entered them for the first time on a fine September morning. The Colonel was a friendly man in his forties, not at all the type one would have expected to be a secret-service man. He was in charge of the section for Preparation for Military Return, a section working in close contact with Military Intelligence, at the head of which was Captain Lieftinck.

Sitting in one of the saddleback armchairs was a large fair man in a naval uniform whom I knew: Quartermaster Bogaart. It turned out that he was there for exactly the same purpose as myself.

I had a look at my surroundings. There was nothing in this bright office room to give the idea that here was one of those centres from which invisible threads ran to our occupied fatherland. I was most impressed. I had as yet no notion of what secret-service work would entail, though I was sure it would be mysterious and romantic. I could not help thinking of the many English detective stories I had read, and I could not quite envisage myself playing the part of the characters in them.

There was nothing very mysterious in what Colonel de Bruyne had to say to Bogaart and myself. Sober reality necessitated certain definite and logical actions. In a business-like way we were told of the dangers of secret-service work and were warned that it was not just a game of Red Indians. And although De Bruyne would be our immediate chief, our actual superiors who would see to our training would be British.

A few moments later two more officers entered the room. One, a small and jovial Englishman, was introduced as Major Blunt, and the other as Captain Bingham. Bingham, who spoke very good Dutch, was a man with an inscrutable expression. The function of neither of these officers was made clear to us, but we took it that they belonged to the British Intelligence Service.

Blunt began to speak of the great dangers involved in the work we were about to undertake. We would probably be dropped in occupied Holland and be given special tasks to perform. If, knowing this, we wished to withdraw, we had better make our minds up quickly; for once we had begun training, withdrawal would be difficult owing to the knowledge we should have acquired concerning secret codes and other details that in no circumstances must leak out. Were we intending to carry on? We were not to think that pressure was being applied. We were as yet free either way.

Bogaart and I exchanged one look and with one voice said, "We're carrying on, Major."

Blunt gave an approving nod and began pacing up and down the room. "That's O.K., then."

Bogaart and I were taken to separate rooms. We were to choose different names, beginning with our own initial letters. I selected Diepenbroek and Bogaart picked Bleker. From the moment our training started our real names were taboo. We were not to mention them to anyone, in case German agents in England should hear of them. We were then told to go to a certain hotel and hold ourselves in readiness for a telephone call. We were to avoid old friends. Was that clear?

A moment later Bogaart and I were standing on the sunny pavement of Park Street. Thoughtfully we strolled to our new hotel. A new life was opening before us. We had said "Yes", and we did not intend to back out. Our fate would be linked with that of the unknown many who did their work in secret. We were puzzled and curious more than anything else.

Three days went by before the telephone call came; three very long days during which we mainly stayed indoors and yawned as we gazed out on to the rainswept street. Instructions were to pack a case with personal belongings and to be at Marble Arch Underground Station at ten o'clock, where a car would pick us up. We were there at nine forty-five. On the stroke of ten the car drew up. We were driven to a naval depot, where we had to hand in our uniforms in exchange for British uniforms with sergeants' stripes.

"Pleased to meet you, Sergeant Diepenbroek," I murmured to myself as I grinned at my reflection in the mirror.

We left the depot and were taken by car out of London to the town of Reading. The scenery was splendid; the autumnal parkland alternated with sloping meadows, and I could easily imagine it as the setting for stage-coaches and hunting meets. Nothing in it led me to think of the existence of a Special Training School, which proved to be one of those stately country mansions, set in a park, far from any public road and almost off the map.

At that time there were only two other trainees, both Dutch. They called themselves Van de Brand and Van Oosterom. Much water was to flow under the bridge before I learned their real names: Van der Bor and Van Os. We were to be trained as one group, and we kept a fairly large staff busy from early morning until late at night.

The training was indeed "special". Out of bed at half-past six and straight on to half an hour's physical exercises, either indoors or out in the open air. Then breakfast, theory and practice, lunch, and again instruction until dinner-time. After a day or so of this I felt as if all my bones had been broken and my brains were bursting out of my head.

For four weeks we were trained in the use of automatic light firearms, in blowing up small objects with explosive charges, in learning radio signals and map-reading, and in sport—a great deal of sport.

Not only were there instructors in all these different subjects but there was also an English sergeant who was taking the course with us. He was of Belgian origin and spoke Antwerp Flemish with an English accent. He was our guardian angel, so to speak, and never left us for a moment. If we were allowed an evening off he would come with us to make sure we did not say anything rash to outsiders. In this friendly way we were taught to guard our tongues—one of the most important factors of our training. He was also there to see that we did not drink a glass too many and that we were not drawn into conversation with inquisitive strangers if we did relax our guard.

Halfway through October we began the second stage of our training. The four of us were taken to the north-west coast of Scotland for an intensified commando course. It was the kind given to ordinary soldiers but quicker and more thorough in every way. It took about eighteen hours spent in trains to reach our destination, plus several hours in a motor-boat. It was a wretched, barren countryside, thinly populated; rain fell from a heavy sky that never cleared completely. Though there were few people there were multitudes of sheep. It was a most depressing place.

We were to stay at a single-storied stone hut hidden among man-high bracken. Training became, if that were possible, even more strenuous. Our instructor was a lieutenant of a Scottish regiment, a hard fellow with a spurious cheerfulness. He was tireless and his muscles bulged under his kilt. How he had managed to get so tanned in that climate we could never discover. At night we would crouch round the open fire, exhausted and soaked to the skin with rain. We felt like jungle trackers out of a Jack London novel.

Here man was supreme and we could do what we liked. There was room enough. We learned how to creep into a house and clear the room with one sweep of bullets. We were made to blow up rocks, of which there were plenty around. And we were taught the useful art of "silent killing": how to creep up on an enemy and deal with him in a way that prevented him from uttering a sound.

At last the day came for our grand manœuvre. And, fortunately, for once the weather was dry and clear. The four of us were put into an armoured car and driven some sixty miles. The car stopped suddenly, the Scotsman told us to get out and handed us a list of instructions. Bidding us a genial farewell, he told us to report back at base within three days.

There we stood, feeling rather foolish in the prevailing silence. Near us was a lake shaped like a banana, the water a steely blue, and behind it a range of snow-capped hills. This was the country through which we had to make our way back. One of our instructions was to blow up a bridge, or at any rate fit an explosive charge under it after having captured the guards. We also had to blow up an ammunition dump somewhere. All we had were some tins of food and our heavy equipment.

We finished our rations that same day, after agreeing that we would find something else the next day. We did. We had been looking out for a farm, and our appetites were working up to a fine performance, when suddenly something edible turned up: a deer, which stopped and stared with amazement at the peculiar spectacle we must have offered. A quarter of an hour later we were roasting large hunks of meat over an improvised fire. Our guns had come in useful after all. We had in our time eaten tenderer meat, but we weren't feeling particular.

Nourished, we went on. At a given point we were supposed to scatter and proceed singly. Hardly had I started out alone before I came to an isolated farm where a fair-haired peasant girl was milking a cow—a scene that was more to my liking than the rest of the landscape. She was the farmer's daughter and her eyes were of an unusual violet-blue colour. A charming girl. How could such a wretched countryside have produced such a girl, I wondered. My fatigue fell from me and I was only too willing to help her catch a few straying sheep, after which she took me to the farm and I was given succulent food by the plateful. The mother, though, was a little suspicious of the tall, strange-looking foreigner; she made it clear that she thought I intended to run off with her daughter. And one could have done worse, I give her that. When the time came for me to set off again, the daughter offered to see me on my way. Our leave-taking was quite lengthy, lost as we were among the tall bracken. It occurred to me that we must have looked like an old-fashioned picture: Shepherd and Shepherdess. After this pleasant interlude I went on my way, looking back at intervals to wave. It was an incident that I did not include in my report upon my return to base.

CHAPTER 9

OPERATION SPROUT

WHEN OUR commando training in the Scottish Highlands came to an end we were transferred to the considerably less romantic setting of Ringway Aerodrome near Manchester. Here we were to be taught the art of parachute jumping. This was the more sensational part of our training, and none of us felt too happy about it.

For the first week we did gymnastics, and again gymnastics, and more gymnastics, to strengthen our leg muscles. The second week we were taken to a hangar containing a number of platforms, each about eighty feet high. We had to climb to the top, where we were hooked to a thin steel cable fixed to some kind of brake and told to jump. We jumped, and rarely have I known such stark fear as I felt at that moment. Eighty feet is a fair height, and if the brake were to fail it would be just too bad for you. But the brake never did fail; it was a wonderful piece of apparatus, and in the end we had grown quite fond of it. It was so adjusted that we touched ground at the exact speed of a parachutist. Before long we were all enjoying it as a novel sport and our stomachs had ceased their agonizing contraction. At this station we were no longer by ourselves but together with men from a variety of services and nations who all, for some reason or other, had to learn the art of parachute jumping.

One day we were hauled up in a large box attached to a

barrage balloon, the box containing four men and one instructor. I had never been up in the air before and enjoyed the new experience. The balloon was held at about six or seven hundred feet up, and I was struck by the eerie silence as we rose. There was not even the noise of an engine as there is in an aeroplane. The only sound was the gentle soughing of the wind through the cables, and one's words seemed to dissolve unheard into space.

I looked down, and my courage suddenly dwindled to nothing. I'll never dare, I thought to myself; yet the instructor was quite calm, and my companions appeared quite calm, though I suspected that their calm was as brittle as mine. As with most things, when you are alone you hesitate, but with others watching you go on, if only to conceal from the watchers how scared you are. Later on, you have a good laugh over the discovery that everyone was feeling exactly the same.

The worst part was the waiting for the first jump. A thousand thoughts ran through my mind and irrelevant images appeared to my mind's eye: my native Walcheren, a cigarette, the Mediterranean sun, a tavern in Den Helder. At last the moment came to jump. I knew a few seconds of alarm, followed by a moment of surprise as I floated through the air like a huge bird. All fear had left me and I was filled with a sense of immense relief, of immense freedom. And pride. The air whistled past my ears and the objects on the ground were rapidly nearing. And then suddenly, breaking the all-enveloping stillness, came the booming of a loudspeaker issuing landing instructions.

Landing is perhaps the most difficult part of parachute jumping. The speed with which one reaches the ground approximates one's natural speed on jumping from a height of ten to twelve feet. The wind must be behind one on landing, for it is easier to come down on one's face than on one's back. The parachute cannot be manipulated, of course, but by pulling the cords in a certain way one can turn oneself right round.

During the next few days I made seven jumps from a Whitley bomber which had been specially constructed for parachute work, with a round hole in the cabin through which the parachutist had to drop. One of my seven jumps was made in the dark, for I was going to be dropped in Holland under cover of night.

From Ringway I went to a school near Beaulieu in southern England, where we were taught the safety measures that must be familiar to an agent. This training was altogether along practical lines, and from the moment that we entered the establishment we had to pretend that we were German agents in Britain. At any moment we might be submitted to interrogation and we had to have a story pat, our "cover story". And we all had to tell the same story. The phrase "at any moment" was the literal truth; we would be woken up in the middle of the night, separated, and each interrogated about what we had done the night before from, say, six o'clock to ten. The one thing we were not allowed to tell was what had actually happened, which meant that we had constantly to agree among ourselves on a story of what we were supposed to have done. The whole art lay in making our stories agree. This preparation of a cover story was gone over until we were sick of it, but we were told that it was a sound method of outwitting German interrogators.

We were also trained in making contact with people whom we knew only from description. We would be told that a man answering to the following particulars would be getting out of a train at such and such a time and place.

We had to go to the station and shadow the man for an hour or so and then report on his actions.

Another item in our curriculum was practice in the use of radio codes and varieties of secret writing. We learned how to set booby traps, especially in the shape of pens and pencils that could be surreptitiously placed on the desks of high-ranking enemies.

To crown the course came a five-day exercise during which we were to act independently. Having been provided with false papers and a roll of money, we were each directed to a town and told to act the part of a German spy. I was given Swansea and told to report on the number of vessels in port, with complete details of cargo, destination and armaments. Secondly, I had to find and prepare a suitable receiving area for dropping containers with arms. All that my chiefs were to know was the name of the hotel at which I was staying; this secrecy was for the benefit of the British counter-espionage, whose personnel did not know that I had been given this particular assignment, so that my test was a test of their efficiency as well.

I was surprised at the usefulness of my training; it was remarkable how many important items of information I was able to gather when I set about it the right way. I spent most of the first day working out my cover story, paying special attention to details that would have to be brought up to date day by day. Before going to the docks, therefore, I made for a cinema and, walking into the entrance hall, studied the pictures and bought a ticket, making sure to attract the cashier's attention in so doing. Having watched the film for about half an hour, I left, unnoticed, by a side entrance. The second day I was tapped on the shoulder by a detective, who took me to a police station for interrogation. I had my story pat and nothing could be charged against me; yet they clearly regarded me as a suspicious character and spent a lot of time examining my false identity papers.

They let me go, and the first thing I did was to steal another set of identity papers. It was surprisingly easy. I went straight to a bar, and within ten minutes I was in conversation with a man who obviously felt lonely. By the third drink he was showing pictures of his wife and children, who lived in another part of the country. He put his wallet on the table, and I studied the pictures long and carefully during two more drinks. Then his identity-card, which stuck out of his wallet, was in my pocket. I left a happy man who had told me all about his family. I altered some details and adopted the name that was on his papers. I went to another hotel and informed my chiefs of this change of domicile; but, as I had now changed both my name and address, counter-espionage must have lost all trace of me, for I had no further encounters with them.

After three of my allotted five days had gone by I had established fairly accurately what ships were in harbour and which of them were going out with the next convoy, with full details. I had even spent a night on board one of the ships after going on a celebration with some of the sailors. For the public-house proved unquestionably the secret agent's best hunting-ground, especially if he can stand rounds of drinks and contrive to stay sober himself.

At the appointed time I returned to Beaulieu and made my report. The particulars I set down were found to be correct, so I had carried out my task to perfection. I was told I had reason to be pleased with myself, as I had been in the hands of the British counter-espionage and had outwitted their vigilance—a rare achievement.

In January 1943 I was sent to a finishing school, where

I was once more taken through the entire curriculum of my training. The final touches were put to my efficiency. With a code specialist I had to work out a security-check —that is to say, a means of sending a radio message in such a way that the British Secret Service, receiving it, would know whether the message had actually been sent by me or not. This sort of security-check is usually a definite kind of error introduced into the text of the message. I was told that should I fall into German hands I was allowed to let them force me to divulge the radio code, but on no account was I to reveal the existence of a security-check; for if the Germans were to use my sender and transmit false messages with my code, the absence of the security-check would clearly signify to the receiving end that I was no longer at liberty.

By the time we were halfway through February I was told to hold myself in readiness. I had passed through so hair-raising a sequence of experiences that the news that I was to be parachuted into occupied territory roused little new excitement in me. I was to be dropped about three miles south of the Dutch town of Ermelo. The place was situated about thirty miles north of Arnhem in one of the rare large stretches of wooded country in Holland. It was always difficult to find dropping-places in Holland, the world's most densely populated country, where towns and villages seem to touch one another. At one time nobody knew that there was a German S.S. camp near Ermelo. On one incredible occasion the agent Dessing had been dropped right into this camp and had walked out with a resounding "Heil Hitler" to the guards at the entrance, who had civilly answered his salute. Dessing was dropped blind and had to find his own way to Amsterdam. Things were better organized now, we were told. I would be met by representative members of the underground movement. My special code-name for this expedition was Paul, and the reception committee would know this name, so that if, upon landing, someone addressed me as Paul that would be proof that all was as it should be.

Not a word was said of the purpose of our impending visit. We gathered that once we were in Holland we would be taken to our immediate chief by the underground reception committee. But it was clear where our work would lie. We reckoned that we should have to organize resistance cells within the underground movement and instruct them in the use of arms and explosives on orders from London—in other words, prepare the ground for the coming invasion of the Continent.

This sounded all very vague, but the importance of secrecy had so often been stressed that we did not feel disturbed. The less we knew of the organization on the other side, the less we could tell the enemy if something went wrong. And after our intensive training we felt confident we could cope with anything. We were not afraid of a whole army of Germans. We knew that there would be hundreds of volunteers to join the resistance cells that had to be formed, all eager to learn the best methods for spreading alarm and despondency among the enemy. I had complete trust in my training.

I was now given a very neat civilian outfit, a false Dutch passport (my assumed name was changed to Dijkman), ration cards, and an automatic pistol in case anything should go wrong on landing. Also I was given an address in Switzerland, hidden in the false bottom of a matchbox, which, should I at any time be driven to flight, I should try to reach.

On the face of it everything seemed well arranged. Yet I was beginning to have qualms, for I could see some very large gaps in the scheme. The organization, so pains-takingly careful over certain details, was remarkably slap-dash in others. There was my suit, for instance. Though all marks and labels had been removed from it, it was unmistakably an English suit in cut and style. I also wondered whether the double-bottomed matchbox was not a little too childish, a little too obvious to be used in trying to outwit a cunning and experienced enemy.

During our period of training my colleagues and I had been given days off, days which we could spend in London. And we went wearing our British uniforms, the only clothes we had. This both Bogaart and I thought was extremely careless, for we had many friends in the navy, and in London we could scarcely fail to meet one or more of them; our appearance in British uniforms was bound to cause comment, for it was known that we had been transferred to Colonel de Bruyne for special work. We wondered why we had not been allowed to retain our Dutch naval uniforms so that we could have gone about without attracting attention to ourselves. We knew how talkative some innocent Dutchmen were, and our British uniforms loudly proclaimed the fact that we belonged to that small and exclusive band which was being sent to work in Holland. It was all supposed to be a secret, but such things get around. But when these points struck us we decided that our chiefs must know what they were doing, and why should we worry; we were about to go on our mission in any case. We said goodbye to Van Os and Van der Bor, who had been given a different assignment. The name of our operation was "Sprout", and that was to be the signature of our radio messages.

Much later we learned that "Sprout" was part of a much bigger operation, the so-called "Plan Holland" which aimed at setting up a complete sabotage organization in the country. Many agents had been dropped before us. Only a few would follow us because uncertainty developed as to the success of the project. But nobody had any doubts when we were given our vague orders. We began working out our cover stories, which were left entirely to us. Our main concern was to prevent the Germans from finding out that we had come from England if we were caught. I had left Holland almost two years before, and things must have changed greatly. I realized that I could not make a good cover story before I had spent a few days in Holland and had been able to familiarize myself with the changed conditions there.

We were now waiting only for good weather and a full moon, and we spent the intervening days at an isolated country house near the aerodrome from which we were to depart. These were days of great nervous tension. Every afternoon we hastened to the blackboard where notices were posted to see whether we were to be dropped during the coming night or not.

Men of various nationalities were staying at this country house; of these, only the Norwegians were fully armed and in uniform, ready to take part in the guerilla warfare in their native mountains. There were also several French girls, for whom we had the greatest admiration. If the training had been hard for us men, how much worse must it have been for these young women.

Towards the end of February a notice appeared that Operation Sprout was to take place that night, and that it would include a third member of our team, one Van Arendse. We drew lots for the order of jumping, and as usual I lost, which meant that I was to be first, Bogaart second, and Arendse third. We made our last preparations, silent, preoccupied, and a little nervous. I spent half an hour searching for something I had in my pocket all the time. And now, I thought, here I am going back to all that hateful suspense from which I escaped two years ago. It was almost unimaginable.

Towards nightfall Captain Lieftinck arrived. He came to give us a farewell dinner and take us to the aerodrome. Things were beginning to move and our excitement was growing. We talked of a host of matters.

One more check-up, to make sure our pockets contained nothing incriminating. Even the tobacco dust of English cigarettes had to be removed. We were carrying very little. The aforementioned matchbox (a well-known Dutch brand: Molentje), a Dutch pencil, a wallet and ration cards, one or two innocent photographs, and an identity card which later proved to be no masterpiece of forgery.

A car took us to the aerodrome; we put on flying overalls and strapped on our parachutes. It was cold and our faces looked grey. Like robots, we tottered across the grass to the aeroplane, a four-engined Halifax bomber, which, sombre and menacing, stood waiting for us. The crew were standing around, their hands in their pockets, smoking last cigarettes. From the accent of their "Hallos" we reckoned they were Poles. They looked at us with envious admiration. The second pilot came up to me and said, "The Germans have murdered my father and my brother. My mother is in a concentration camp. If you ever have the chance of shooting down a couple of S.S. men or Green men, do it for my sake, will you? Promise me that, Dutchman; it'll make me happier."

There were a good many O.K.s and cheerios and au revoirs. We climbed in and the door slammed behind us. Not a word was said. I heard the engines start up, one after the other. One period of my life was closing, a new chapter was opening: one of hunting and being hunted, of tension and lurking danger—perhaps of torture and a firing-squad.

Before I had thought all that, the beat of the engines was beginning to quicken. I looked out of a window and saw the lights of the runway shooting past us. A few moments later we were airborne. Well, I thought, I've gone into this with my eyes open, and of my own free will. And I'll have to go on to the end, bitter or not.

CHAPTER 10

THIRD TIME LUCKY

THE HALIFAX was flying low to give the enemy detecting apparatus as little warning as possible. The white moonlight was dancing on the waves of the empty North Sea; not a ship was to be seen. In silence we waited, and after about an hour we heard that the Dutch coastline was in sight. Now we were gaining height, and before long we saw the white line of the surf and the greyish sand-dunes gliding beneath us. One or two searchlights were pointing in the sky like crossed bean-poles. This was Holland. I was surprised to find that I felt no emotion whatsoever.

A member of the crew opened the jumping-hatch and shouted "Get ready, number one" into my ear. A cold stream of air blew through the hole as I sat on the edge, my legs dangling in space. Looking down, I saw the waters of the Ysselmeer beneath me, the former Zuyder Zee. I could not suppress a shiver. It had just gone midnight. We were to be over the dropping area at twelve-fifteen. Over the town of Harderwijk, I threw down a bag of V-shaped sweets in accordance with instructions. This was intended to mask the real purpose of our flight from the Germans.

The ground looked misty as we flew over the central sandy plain of the Veluwe, with the town of Apeldoorn somewhere on the right. To think that two years before I had been walking about there in the uniform of a *maréchaussée*! The plane began to circle.

"Here we are!"

I was tensely watching the little red lamp above my head, for the moment it switched to green was the moment for me to jump. My feet were growing numb with cold, and it was an effort to keep my legs still in the strong current of air. This was lasting a long time, far too long. My eyes were beginning to ache with staring at the red light, and my nerves were growing steadily worse. After a very long time a voice spoke in my ear. "No good. We can't see the lights of the reception committee on account of this damned ground mist. We're going back."

The tension had been too great; it had lasted too long. I couldn't say a word. My teeth were chattering.

At a quarter to two we were back over our starting-point in England, which we had left less than three hours earlier. I could hardly believe that within a quarter of an hour we'd be having a whisky in the messroom. Objects were becoming clearer, the plane touched down, the roar of the engines died away, and it seemed very quiet. I had the feeling that this unsuccessful expedition had affected me more than the whole of my Mediterranean experiences. This was England, free England. We did not know whether to feel relief or not.

"Hallo, hallo! No good?"

"No, total failure. Ground mist."

"Better luck next time."

"Yes, I hope so."

We had our drink. The mess-boy greeted us as old friends. I told my two companions that one of them would have to go first next time. I'd had my share.

The "next time" was not long postponed. It came within twenty-four hours. The same farewells were said, and into the plane we climbed. But this time our nerves were steadier. We had a British crew, and warm sleeping-bags had been provided. I had a pleasant nap. When we were just off the Dutch coast I was woken by a member of the crew, and, looking out of the window at which he was pointing, I saw searchlights and tracer bullets. Suddenly we were caught in the beam of one of the searchlights and a network of glowing, hissing serpents enveloped us, giving us a strangely helpless feeling.

We were, it appeared, over the island of Texel at about one thousand five hundred feet. I tried in vain to make out the contours of the land, the lights were too blinding. I found myself praying that this was not the end.

At first it seemed that my prayers were not going to be heard. A shock passed through the plane as we were hit. The pilot was taking frantic evasive action; in sharp bends and dives and climbs he was trying to escape from the searchlight beams. He succeeded in that, but I could see a red glow on the port side which meant that one of the engines was on fire. The order was given, "Stand by for baling out." The pilot directed the plane to a considerable height and then dived in an attempt to extinguish the flames by excessive draught, and this also was successful. But the engine was coughing badly and had to be taken out of action, which meant stopping one of the starboard engines as well. On two engines we limped back to England.

Third time lucky, we said.

Five days later we were called to London. Poker-faced Captain Bingham told us that in the normal course of events we should have had to wait another three weeks before making another attempt, for the phase of the full moon was over. But there were reasons why we should go earlier. Were we prepared to make our jumps in the dark without the aid of moonlight? It would be more dangerous, as the moment of landing and the nature of the ground could be judged less easily. Since it was all in a good cause, we declared ourselves willing to try.

On this same occasion I had a discussion with one of the security experts, who had pointed out that the security-check of my radio code was too similar to another agent's. We discussed the necessary modification very agreeably.

On the night of March 9th to 10th, 1943, we made a third attempt. I was sure we should make it this time, and my nerves did not disturb me in the least. We had a fine trip, crossed the Ysselmeer as before, passed Harderwijk and released a dozen carrier-pigeons, each in a small wicker basket attached to a parachute, and each carrying a request to the patriotic finder to write any important information on the slips in the small tube tied to the bird before letting it fly home.

The order came, "Action! Action! Make ready to jump." Bogaart was number one this time, I was number two, and Arendse number three. Before I had had much time for brooding the green light glowed. Bogaart vanished through the hole.

Someone gave me an encouraging pat on the shoulder, and I, too, jumped. I hurtled down at what seemed a colossal speed and at last felt a wrench as the parachute opened. The roar of the aeroplane engine died away and I was falling in dead silence. There were few stars; below me I could see flashes of light, the agreed signal of the reception committee. As quickly as I could, I made out my bearings and reckoned I would land about two-thirds of a mile south of them.

The ground was still invisible; below me was nothing but inky blackness and it was impossible to estimate height. Suddenly something lashed my face and I felt a violent shock. I was caught in a tree. How far down was the ground? I dropped my helmet and listened: a negligible distance. I unstrapped my parachute and let myself drop, falling about six or eight feet. At that moment I heard the aeroplane returning, circling the area a second time. I felt an understandable longing to be back on that small speck of freedom so far above me. I now knew myself to be one of the eight million Dutch who were cut off from the free world beyond Holland's shores.

In the distance I could hear voices and I saw some vacillating lights approaching. Probably the right people, but I wasn't prepared to take risks. I hid in the bushes and waited, my finger on the trigger of my pistol. Twigs snapped nearby. I was crouching on one knee in dead leaves and could smell the fresh bark of oak trees.

Then I heard my code-name being called, "Paul! Paul!" That was good enough. I stepped forward and walked up to them.

Two men stood facing me, to be joined a moment later by a third. Their welcome was hearty and their manner jovial. We shook hands and they told me that they were taking me straight to the leader of the reception committee. It was about a quarter of an hour's walk, to the edge of the woods. They had already found my two colleagues, who had both landed unharmed.

We made our way through the undergrowth and before long saw some lamp signals in the distance. These people are being very lavish with their lights, I thought to myself. A few moments later we reached the rest of the reception committee and Bogaart and Arendse. The leader welcomed me and explained that we had another two hours to wait before we could get to Ermelo, where we were to meet the chief. We were given some English cigarettes, which were clearly a legendary luxury, and a nip of whisky from flasks. Items of news and information were exchanged.

We spoke in whispers, my colleagues and I expressing our jubilation at having made at last a successful landing. After half an hour the leader said it was time to be on the move and we had better take no risks of endangering anyone. Would we hand over our weapons to him; he would keep them safe and hand them back to us later. We might at one point have to pass Germans, and if we were found to be carrying arms the situation might become awkward. That seemed reasonable to us. The leader took charge of our pistols and of the fourteen containers of high explosive that had been dropped after us. They were to be transported along another route. He then began to tell us that the identity papers being issued from England of late had been shockingly bad. The other day two men had been caught on that very account. Could he see ours? He inspected them carefully by the light of his torch and shook his head. "It's a disgrace, sending you fellows over with such rubbish," he commented indignantly. "These are suicidal, they smell to heaven of forgery."

He handed back our papers, telling us to keep them for the present, and he would see about getting us better ones later. Then, apparently as an afterthought, he added, "But you'll have to give us your real names. Those identity cards with phoney names are no good. When you get to a post where they are at all thorough, one phone call proves them wrong. You will have to have names off the national register and then you'll be all right. But I think you'd better work under your own names in any case."

This again seemed fairly reasonable, but Bogaart, Arendse and I decided to have a word with each other about it. We drew to one side and had a long discussion. We had been told on no account to divulge our real names, but circumstances seemed somewhat abnormal here. There had obviously been some slipshod work at H.Q. And people on the spot were likely to know better. So we acquiesced and told them what they wanted to know.

It was about four o'clock in the morning when the signal was given for us to move; the morning air was chilly and the trees were covered with hoar frost. We split up into small groups, each of us three being accompanied by two men of the reception committee. The groups were about a hundred yards apart and we were told to keep absolutely silent.

After about five minutes my two companions suddenly hurled themselves upon me, pinning my arms behind my back. I heard the click of handcuffs. The attack had been so quick that I had offered no resistance, and in any case I thought they were being funny. "Don't start larking about now," I told them, but one of the men roughly prodded a revolver into my back. A whistle blew and a number of men emerged from the bushes around and surrounded us.

One of them peered into my face. "Well, well," he said. "So you thought you'd be clever and jump from an English plane, did you? And come and do some sabotage here, eh? You're not going to like it, my friend. You've been caught by the German counter-espionage. You'll never hear those explosives going off now. You've been betrayed and we've got the whole of your organization in our hands." All this was said in perfect Dutch.

I was too taken aback to speak. The whole structure of my plans and hopes had collapsed. At last I found words. "In our hands—*our* hands? What do you mean, you dirty Judas? Think you're a German, do you? Come on, then, shoot, you coward."

"No," the other replied. "That is just what we're not going to do. First, you're going to tell us all you know. The war's over for you. You've had it. If you do what we tell you nicely you'll stay alive and well."

I swore surpassingly well, very fluently, and, of course, to no purpose. I found it difficult to credit that there were such traitors in the whole wide world, such loathsome, fawning slaves of the Nazis. My captors seemed to be feeling a little embarrassed, for they began to trot out weak excuses, about trying to safeguard our people from reprisals, for instance. It was so obviously parrot talk, obediently repeated. The only satisfaction I had, among those frosty trees, was telling them that the day would come when they would be put in rows against a wall, and then . . .

They did not like that much, and in silence took us to a road where three cars and a lorry were waiting. Our containers were loaded on to the lorry and carefully hidden under camouflage nets. They seemed to have everything well organized. Meanwhile the manacled Bogaart and Arendse had arrived. Each was pushed into a different car with a guard sitting on either side. It was growing mistier, and I thought it might be worth while to make an attempt at escaping. I had nothing to lose. I was bound to be shot in the end, whatever happened, so I might as well sell my life for a good price.

As we threaded our way along the byroads, I found that my handcuffs were fairly loose and that I might be able to ease my right hand out. I had an excellent fighting knife in my boot, and it would be an exquisite pleasure to me to send these traitors to kingdom come and escape in their car. But just as my hand came free and my fingers were about to close round the handle of my knife my elbow nudged my neighbour, who leapt up. The man behind me pressed his revolver against the back of my neck and the two sitting beside me fell upon me and pinned me down. I had had very little room to move. The handcuffs were fastened on my wrists again and I was made to put my hands on the back of the seat in front of me. My only reward was that my captors had gone white with fear.

CHAPTER II

A PLAN

IT WAS half-past five by the time the fleet of cars drew up outside a villa at Driebergen, a small town a few miles west of Utrecht. It was still dark and we were pushed along a garden path. A door opened, a flood of yellow light poured out over the tiled porch, and a moment later we were standing in the bright hall, facing a martial portrait of the Führer. There seemed to be considerable excitement in the house. Doors were being slammed, and the buzz of subdued voices filled the house. We were each taken to a separate room.

I was brought before a short, plump German in civvies who began to interrogate me straight away, while another man thoroughly searched me. The short man seized upon my matchbox and without any hesitation detached the false bottom and triumphantly waved the small slip of paper bearing the Swiss address.

"Perhaps you'll kindly decipher this for me," he said in broken Dutch.

I pretended ignorance. The man laughed. "I suppose, if you had managed to escape, you would have gone to Rochussen Street in Rotterdam, wouldn't you?"

It was as if he had struck me a blow in the face, for that was the address I had been given in England as a safe harbour if I failed to make contact with the reception committee. I must have winced, for the German continued to show off his knowledge. He mentioned a number of Dutch and English instructors by name and told me at which schools I had received my training during the last six months, correct in every detail. "You see," he went on, "we know it all. We have our people in England, and I'm sure you know them too. You have been betrayed, and it will be as well for you if you give truthful answers to my questions."

I had no intention of capitulating so easily. "I wish I knew the traitor," I muttered.

"Ah!" the German replied. "His name doesn't matter. We know all about you people." And then came a barrage of questions, mainly concerned with my radio code and my instructions. I declared I had no radio code, that I had been dropped, and that I was to report to the reception committee and take their orders. The interrogation lasted for two hours, by which time my interrogator was getting bored. "If you won't tell me," he said, "I'll take you and prove to you that all your colleagues are in our hands and that your whole organization is run by us."

I was given breakfast, though one of my hands was manacled to the chair. After the meal I was again securely shackled and a blanket was tied round my legs to prevent me from running. I was put on a stretcher, transported by ambulance to Haaren in the province of North Brabant and taken to a large seminary that had been turned into a Gestapo prison. There I was handed over to Herr May, a code specialist.

I was first searched yet more thoroughly; my clothes were inspected as if the searchers were seeking for vermin. And after that the interrogation proper began. May was a typical Prussian, corpulent, his hair clipped short. He put on an act of friendliness and patience, never grew excited, and displayed the notorious German thoroughness.

He was assisted by a young Dutch woman called De Bruin, who acted as his secretary.

I had no wish to let myself be drawn into admissions. In any case I was beginning to feel sleepy. What thoughts I had I concentrated on my experiences of that morning, calculating what my chances would have been if at such or such a point I had hurled myself at my captors. A sudden sharpness in May's voice brought me back to reality. "If you won't listen, I'll soon cure you of your obstinacy." He got up. "Come on," he said. "I'll show you something that will interest you."

We walked through the corridors of the prison and up to the second floor. Soon we stood before a long row of cells, formerly the rooms where young Dutchmen had prepared themselves for the priesthood. Now every room had bars over the skylight and a small spy-hole. "Look, but do not say anything or I shall have to shoot," said May, his gun prodding me in the back. In the first cell there were two young men. "Do you know them?" May asked. I did not. We went on. Soon I saw two faces I recognized. I had seen them on the aerodrome at Ringway near Manchester, where I learned parachute jumping. Then there were two or three others I had seen before. I had met them in hotels where I had stayed during my training. At last I saw my friends Van der Bor and Van Os, with whom I had been trained but who had been dropped before me. There were other men, at least forty. "Some have been here for a year already," May said. I shivered. A year in that prison! Would it not be better to be shot immediately? Wild thoughts raced through my mind. Should I try to knock this German out and escape. They lasted only a second, however, because I was demoralized. I had no strength left for action.

[106]

The ghastly truth was inescapable. May gave me a glance full of meaning and led me downstairs again for further interrogation. He began by asking me to decode the address that had been hidden in the matchbox. I made some pretence at trying, and then said there must be a mistake in it as I couldn't work it out. May smiled. "Give it to me," he said. "If you won't do it I will." He decoded it immediately and correctly. "You mustn't be so headstrong, Zeelander; it won't get you anywhere."

I was beginning to feel that we had been betrayed even before we had left England, and that feeling had the effect of lowering my resistance. The interrogation went on and on, and I was allowed no sleep. When I dozed off, I was shaken awake and more questions were hurled at me. There were dozens of them, all showing a thorough familiarity with the working of our organization. But that was not the only thing that interested them. They wanted to know when I had gone to England, who had helped me to escape from Holland. "We do not want to arrest these people; we only want to know the escape-lines," they said. The wolves did not want to eat the, lambs! They wanted information about my illegal work before my departure. By whom had I been helped? Every careless answer could send people to their deaths. But on these points they did not insist too much. It was easy to tell them a few lies, and they never talked about these matters again. England and everything connected with my training and operational orders were of the greatest interest. By whom had I been questioned when I arrived in England and what had I been asked? For a moment I thought that it might be harmless to answer such questions. But then it flashed through my mind that they could send their own people to England and that, armed with this information, they would pass the security-tests.

May was even interested in the ground-plan and furniture of the rooms in the Patriotic School. He wanted me to make a sketch of the building. I did not remember enough, I could answer truthfully. Was not there a man at the Patriotic School who had tried to buy the valuable objects I had on me? I had had none, but I remembered that some men who had arrived from Holland had complained that one of the officers of the school had tried to buy their gold rings cheap.

When I decided to give information it was clear that it was not new to the German. It was also clear that he knew considerably more than I did. In replying to a question about the appearance of a certain officer I described him as a clean-shaven man. "If that is so," May commented, "he must have changed his appearance. A fortnight ago he still wore a fine handlebar moustache."

I remembered then that the man under discussion had had a moustache and was always twiddling the ends of it. It was staggering. There must be a colossal leakage somewhere, but where? How was it possible? I was groping in the dark. And May smiled more and more. But I wasn't going to give him my radio code. Not yet, at any rate. The interrogation went on continuously for forty hours.

Slowly I became conscious of a new danger. Every time I told the truth the German made a deprecatory gesture and added information which sometimes I knew, and sometimes I didn't know. I felt inclined to show him that there were a few things he did not know, but I managed to resist this impulse. I felt that I needed a cigarette and asked whether I could have one. "You can have all the cigarettes you want when you have answered the questions," was the answer. Herr May did not mal-treat me, he hardly ever shouted, and seemed to be proud of his moderate behaviour. "You did not expect such fair treatment from the Gestapo?" he asked. I remained silent. "There are many things the British have not told you," he said. I was inclined to admit that this was true, but did not answer.

At last I was taken to a solitary cell, where I dropped on the hard bench and was sound asleep in seconds. Hardly had I woken up the next day before a guard came to fetch me for another interrogation. May was still very friendly. He spoke for some time about the consequences of sabotage to the Dutch people. In Haaren prison there were many Dutch hostages, people of rank and position, many of whom were known through the whole country. "Five were shot when a railway was blown up by some misguided people like you. By answering our questions you can protect your own people. The Queen herself does not like this sabotage business." I laughed. "How do you know?" I asked. "By now it should be clear to you that we know many things that you do not even suspect," he answered. "Nonsense," I said, and May smiled, certain of his superior knowledge. "Your col-leagues have had more sense than you have," he said. He asked whether I was afraid of being executed. There he could dispel my fears. Himmler himself and the highest authorities had promised that the agents that were dropped and captured would be treated as prisoners of war. They would not be court-martialed. The war was over for them, and after the war they would be released. He looked at me to see whether this was making an impression. Perhaps it might have done if I had believed him, but Nazi promises were of little value even when given with a smiling face.

Then he resumed his interrogation. As before, it took him a long time before he came to the point. He wanted my code and security-check, but for a long time he asked me questions about agents of other nationalities. Had I ever met any Belgian or French agents? I had not. He behaved as though it was not very important. "You saw your colleagues in prison here. There are such prisons in France and Belgium." Then he talked about my training in sabotage. He was a code specialist himself but seemed to know a lot about sabotage, in which I considered myself a bit of an expert. Slowly he tried to build up an atmosphere of confidence between us. We were two men discussing a subject in which we were both interested. I could find no serious objections to telling him a few of our tricks because I knew that they were also taught in German sabotage schools. May was pleased, but he never admitted that there was anything new in my information. He even managed to indicate that the British were rather backward in that field. And again I felt the urge to tell him something that would shake him. But I never forgot one fact: the man facing me was my enemy, even though he had given me a few cigarettes. However, nothing could be lost by being friendly, if May wanted to play that game. Suddenly, when he thought that I was in the right mood, he switched again to the matter of codes and security-checks.

So it went on, day after day. Sometimes we spoke about Scotland, sometimes about Beaulieu. Occasionally May told me an interesting fact about the young women in our organization. He told stories about Blunt and Bingham and knew a lot about the habits of my Dutch chiefs. I could not get accustomed to it, and every time he showed his knowledge I felt as though a cold hand had gripped my heart. This game continued for some six weeks, and I decided that the time had come for me to reveal my radio code.

"Well, well," the German yawned. "So you're showing signs of intelligence at last. Not that I didn't know your code, but we like to have it confirmed at first hand. Give it, and then we'll have your security-check."

"Right," I said, pretending I was past caring. But I had a plan. I gave my code and then the rejected security-check, the one I had been told to discard just before I left. That can do no harm, I thought. And I noticed that May seemed pleased and quite unsuspicious. It was unlikely that he should be suspicious, for the discarded security-check had been entirely in keeping with the rules of the code and could easily have been the right one. I thought that I had fooled May. If the Germans started sending telegrams to England in my code it would immediately be realized that they did not come from me. They did try. Soon they were sending fake messages in this code, probably asking for sabotage material for the resistance cells that we were supposed to be organizing. Nobody noticed anything suspicious in England in spite of the fact that the check on these messages was wrong. They continued to drop agents, and the containers with material went on arriving even when no more agents were being sent. The joke was on me.

For the weeks that the interrogation lasted I was kept alone in a cell. The treatment I received, on the whole, was not bad. Food was fairly plentiful, and I was even allowed a weekly tobacco ration. I spent the time when I was not being grilled in May's office lying stretched out on the bench watching the smoke curling from my diminutive cigarettes. I pondered long and hard, trying to see the flaw in our system. It was clear that there had been treachery. But where? From certain remarks that May had dropped, I was aware that the radio communications with England were in German hands.

After a few days I had succeeded in establishing contact with my neighbours by tapping on one of the radiator pipes. One of them was Van Os, the other a man who called himself De Wilde. We carried on endless conversations in Morse, exchanging views and suspicions but coming no nearer a solution. It wasn't likely that we should so long as we were incarcerated there.

In Haaren prison there was hardly any other subject of conversation. Day and night the discussions raged in the cells round this topic: how did the Germans manage their great coup? If all of us had been together in one big cell and we had been able to pool our information it might not have been difficult to solve the riddle. Now we were hopelessly on the wrong track thanks to the Germans, who skilfully encouraged the idea that there was treason on the English side. They even suggested the identity of the traitor, and so day after day the walls of the prison resounded with the name of an English officer, a man who was completely innocent. What few of us realized was that the little bits of information which we gave built up an exact picture which the Germans used to bluff their next victims. Some colleague told May that Captain X had a handlebar moustache, thinking that it was an absolutely useless piece of information. But when it was used on me I was staggered. If the Germans knew things like that, what was the use of obstinate resistance. The most horrible idea that struck me in these weeks was that this game had probably been going on for months without the authorities on our side suspecting a thing. It was no use talking about a solution. We had to establish contact with the authorities in England—but how? How could we escape from our captivity? One might as usefully try to bring the dead back to the realms of the living. And yet it seemed to be our only chance.

I found it difficult to put any trust in the promises the Germans made me: that we would be treated as prisoners of war and not as spies. I was convinced that they would keep us alive as long as we were useful to them, as long as they thought they could get information out of us, but would execute us as soon as we were squeezed dry. Every morning, when I was woken up by the sound of my cell door being flung open, my first thought was: the firing-squad. Those six weeks in solitary confinement were very long weeks. The suspense of this uncertain waiting for death played havoc with my nerves. My sleep was never deep, and I would start awake in terror, bathed in sweat. I would stare into the darkness, light a cigarette, or eat a slice of stale bread. Telling myself to be strong-minded, I would go to the window, pull myself up by the bars and gaze out. Spring had come. I heard the song of birds and could smell, drifting on the night air, the sweet scent of the new grass in spite of the prevailing lysol stench. I listened to the regular tread of the sentries and watched the beams of searchlights raking the skies, throwing the bars of my cell into sharp relief. My thoughts returned to my youth. I saw our living-room clearly before my eyes, my father reading the newspaper, my mother darning socks. I realized now how hard my parents had worked to give their three sons a decent education and what sadness I had often caused them through thoughtlessness, coming home with torn clothes or broken clogs. I remembered one afternoon when we had a holiday from school and I was supposed to be helping my father lift potatoes. But I hadn't felt like lifting potatoes and had run away to play with my schoolmates instead.

Then my first job: looking after the cows that grazed along the sea-dyke. I used to sit staring out to sea and envying my two brothers who were both in the marines. And my next job: a farm labourer. The back-aches from bending and tilling while just beyond the dykes was the calling sea. My father would say, "Two boys in the navy, that's more than enough. You are going to stay ashore."

But one day, when I was sixteen, I told my master that he could do the job himself and I ran away. Before long I enlisted and became an ordinary seaman on the depot-ship in Flushing. The first time I came home on leave, with my hair cut so short that it was almost shaved, my elder brothers teased me by calling me a naked deck-swabber and I retorted by calling them striped jazz-beetles. From the depot-ship I was transferred to the *Gelderland*, a venerable craft, which in its Boer War days had given refuge to Paul Krüger. She was a coal-burner, and the coal in those days had to be taken to the bunkers in wheelbarrows. I remembered the hot quayside and the coal dust; and the barrel-organ playing patriotic tunes. And then my first trip out, to the Canaries, when I had been seasick for a week and had doubted the wisdom of going to sea.

All these recollections passed before my mind as, in the solitude of my cell, death seemed to be lurking round the corner. At times I wished those days could be re-called, that I might have another chance to lift potatoes and look after cows on the sea-dyke. But there was no return; there never is. And, in any case, I was a secret agent; I had been caught in war-time and I could see no reason why I should not suffer the fate that awaited every captured spy.

No, the only hope lay in escape, and I had to think of a way of getting out of my prison. I had to warn them in

England and end this terrible fiasco, even if it cost me my life. Not that I was going to throw my life away for nothing. I would think and ponder until a solution came to me.

After some six weeks they ceased interrogating me. I was moved to another cell, where, to my great delight, I found Bogaart. I asked him what he thought were the chances of escape, but he shook his head. "Suicidal," he said. "Before you'd taken three steps you would be shot down. Forget it."

That was scarcely encouraging. The days drifted by in dreary regularity. Get up, eat, exercise, eat, sleep: a monotonous routine. Spring was lovely that year; there were hot days that made the atmosphere in the cell well-nigh unbearable. The quarter of an hour's break in a square surrounded by barbed-wire entanglements was the only relief, not only because it gave us some fresh air but because it afforded me a better idea of our surroundings. I was still nursing hopes of escape. "You never know," I thought. But escape during exercise was patently impossible. We were invariably guarded by a German holding a sub-machine gun ready. Escape from our cell? Bogaart and I were on the first floor and our cell overlooked an inside courtyard patrolled night and day: at night the sentries even took the precaution of playing strong beams of light on our windows. The walls encircling our prison were high and topped with towering barbed wire. At regular intervals around our prison, sentries with searchlights were posted.

All my colleagues suffered from dejection—those at any rate with whom I was in contact through the radiator pipes—but there was a prevailing belief that the German promise not to execute us was genuine. I was still not convinced of that. I was proved right. Almost all my colleagues were killed and the men who had promised to save them disclaimed responsibility. But probably to the end the agents believed that they would survive. After the war I met many ex-prisoners of the Germans. Secretly they had all had one great fear. They had all been certain that they would be shot at the last moment, before the German collapse. But in all camps and prisons it had been bad form to talk about this possibility. Life was hard enough as it was in those places without contemplating violent death at the end. So everybody had pretended that he believed that the Germans would play the game. And after a while many had come to believe it.

From time to time new victims were brought in. Could we not think of some means of warning them in England? Bogaart and I discussed it endlessly. After many abortive attempts we succeeded in establishing communication with prisoners on the floor below us. They were civilian hostages and it appeared that they were able to get messages through to the outside world. Could they get a message over to England for us? Yes, they thought they could. Bogaart and I concocted an S.O.S.: *Entire organization in German hands stop even radio communications stop all agents captured now at Haaren stop Dourlein and Bleker.*

We waited impatiently. It was a long time before an answer came. Our message had gone out and a reply had been received: *Investigations being made.* We sighed with relief; would their eyes be opened at last? We were optimistic enough to hope so.

Our optimism was justified. Our telegram was the first message that reached England telling the authorities that something was wrong. It had suffered considerably in transmission, and our text, which had first gone to a doctor in Haaren prison, had then been smuggled to the

Dutch underground outside and then to the Dutch military attaché in Switzerland, reached our chief, Colonel de Bruyne, in the following form: *Eight parachutists among whom Doulin and Drake were arrested many weeks ago. Codeword Marius known to the enemy.* This was the message that arrived in England on June 23rd, 1943. De Bruyne did not understand it and asked in Switzerland for more information. The military attaché could not help at that moment, but De Bruyne had acted already. He told the British authorities that no more agents should be dropped till the situation was clear.

I learned all this long after the war. Then I realized also that it was an almost incredible piece of luck that our warning had arrived in England. Many others had been sent by members of the Dutch underground. One agent, Dessing, had sent a message from Belgium in which he said that some transmitters of the agents were in German hands. The answer was that Dessing was probably not trustworthy and the Belgians should be cautious in their dealings with him.

In the middle of June we were moved to yet another cell, where Van der Bor joined us. Our meeting was almost rapturous, and soon after we had come together a heavy droning overhead told us that Allied planes were passing over. We saw them, countless silver specks in perfect formations, glittering in the summer sun: Flying Fortresses. Five minutes later our prison was shaking to its foundations. Vast explosions vibrated through the morning air. We three began to shout and sing and were quickly joined by our neighbours, so that a pæan of song rose from the prison. Our guards ran up and down the corridors, shouting and cursing, kicking our doors and rattling their keys, but none of us took any notice of them. We felt grand after this spontaneous outburst. We had been singing as if we had wanted the American airmen to hear us.

Even during the night-time, as the bombers of the R.A.F. came over on their way to Germany, I would stand for hours on the small table by the window, watching them and dreaming of the freedom they symbolized and of the joy it would be to be fighting again for freedom. The relentless drone of the Allied engines filled me with faith and self-confidence, and I began to wage a moral warfare with the guards. I talked a lot to them during exercise-time. Had they heard the bombers over again last night? Where did they think they had been? I would tell them of the preparations I had seen in England. Yes, there would be more and more of these bombers coming now. I wondered whether the guards would ever see their wives and children again. One of them was a pale Sudeten German and he was very impressionable. One day he burst into tears.

"Oh, if only this war would end!"

Two days after I had been moved into my new cell I established contact with our neighbours in the usual way. On one side were Piet de Wilde and Jan Kist, and on the other Overes and Ubbink. Almost my first question was whether they were interested in attempting an escape with me. Ubbink was the only one who immediately agreed, and I asked him to keep his eyes skinned and look out for possibilities. To begin with, we contrived to scrape a small hole in the wall under the wash-basin, which meant we no longer had to use the slow and laborious Morse tapping. For hours we lay on the floor on either side of that hole, whispering in turns into each other's ear.

After about a month we had formulated a plan. We did not imagine for a moment that it was infallible, but we reckoned it had a minute chance of success. We were agreed that it would be better to risk all and perhaps be shot down than to linger in prison for years perhaps, and then be shot by the Germans. All our companions declared us mad, but were prepared to give us any help they could and risk possible reprisals.

Why were they so unenterprising? That is a question that Ubbink and I have often been asked. The answer must be found in their experiences. Their morale was shattered when they were captured by the men whom they thought were their friends. Many had sunk into utter despair during their interrogations when they discovered that there was nothing that the Germans did not know. Some months in a German prison did not improve their stamina. We were well treated, but slowly one's strength of mind ebbed away. Lack of exercise, lack of proper food sapped the will to escape.

Then there was the monotony of prison life, almost soothing in its dullness. At six in the morning we were wakened. We washed and waited for breakfast. We cleaned our cells and waited for lunch at twelve o'clock. Then we began to wait for supper at five-thirty. At 8 p.m. the guards came for a last visit and we had to put our clothes on a chair in the corridor. Half an hour later the lights went out and another day had gone by. That was the regular routine. In theory we went outside for a quarter of an hour's exercise each day, but the Germans had a way of forgetting about this. There was nothing to do but read and talk. The days seemed endless, but for some mysterious reason the weeks seemed short.

We studied all the prison noises: the steps of the guards in the corridors, the voices of the men who worked in the gardens, the rattle of the food-waggon which announced that the time for a meal had come.

Sometimes May or Schreieder, the Gestapo-men, spent a day interrogating the prisoners. This was a sign that the German affairs were not going as they should. They wanted information on some topic. Every time one of the agents was called from his cell to appear before the Germans, there was a feeling of mingled joy and bitterness. We knew that our man would have a difficult time, that they would try to get information from him that would mean prison for others, but at the same time the visit showed that the Germans had their worries.

Generally, however, life was very quiet. Prison even had its compensations. Nowhere else in the occupied territories could one speak freely, because there was always the chance that a traitor would be listening. But in Haaren one could say whatever one liked without fear of arrest.

It was a dull life and dulled the spirit.

After the plan came the preparations. I was glad that I had had my training, which helped me to take all sorts of small factors into consideration. The outside window of the cell looked down upon a heavily guarded courtyard. The window over the door was clearly the only escape route. It had the usual hinged sash, opening inwards. On the corridor side were iron bars. I remembered that one of the instructors at Beaulieu had told us that many prison bars are far enough apart for a man to squeeze through. "You wouldn't think so at first sight," he had said, "and you would think you'd never get through, but often that's nothing but an optical illusion. Never trust your eyes in the matter of prison bars. Take an accurate measurement with a piece of string and then you'll know for certain."

I unpicked a thread from my mattress, stood on a chair under the transom, stretched the thread against the window-pane and carefully measured the distance between the bars. Then I tore a strip off my sheet and tied the broom to the upright at the end of my bed, leaving just the distance I had measured, and began to practise. It was not easy, but I found that if I took my outer garments off I could manage to squeeze through. Difficult but possible.

The window had been nailed down, which was another obstacle. Those nails had to be removed, and that without the help of pincers. All the tools we had were a fork and a spoon. Ubbink and I spent a fortnight on removing the nails, enlarging the holes and loosely putting the nails back, for everything had to retain its normal appearance on account of the occasional cell inspections. Apart from everything else, we had to work on our preparations during the infrequent moments when there were no guards about.

For the final effort we needed a thirty-six-foot rope (the estimated distance of the top floor from the ground) strong enough to take the weight of a man. One day, when we were given shaving apparatus—a twice-weekly event— I cut the cloth on the underside of the mattress into long strips which I plaited in regulation navy fashion. Ubbink agreed to make a similar rope so that, when joined to mine, it could be looped and drawn down after us to delay discovery and prevent too early a realization of our escape.

Bear in mind that Ubbink, up to the time we made contact in prison, had been a complete stranger to me. We had never met in England, nor had we come face to face in the prison, for prisoners were never allowed to meet men from other cells. Our exercise was taken cell by cell. Ubbink and I knew only each other's voices. I had learned that he had been a ship's officer in the merchant navy and was one year younger than myself.

We agreed that the best time to leave our cells was just before supper when the guard was going round with a trolley that made a considerable noise, and the best moment was when he was in the other arm of the horseshoe corridor. Having got out of our own cells, we would have to make our way to an empty cell. We knew there was one just where the corridor turned into the wing in which the guard would be doling out food, for when we were taken out for exercise we had noticed that the door always stood open. When the guard returned with the empty trolley we would tiptoe behind him in stockinged feet and hide in a lavatory which looked out over the courtyard and which, moreover, projected just beyond the barbed-wire exercise enclosure. We should have to wait in that lavatory until approximately midnight, for only then would it be dark enough for us to attempt lowering ourselves out of the window.

There was also a rule that every evening we had to place all our outer garments on a chair outside the cell in order to render escape more difficult, but as Ubbink and I were one of three we reckoned that our guard might be deceived by the amounts put out.

Our plan was obviously one long series of speculations; and at any point it could easily go wrong.

Knowing that there were fewer guards on Saturdays and Sundays, we chose the moonless Sunday night of August 29th.

CHAPTER 12

A FREE ROOF

THAT SUNDAY morning I woke very early, and I got up and looked out of the window. In spite of the early hour it was already oppressively hot, and my nerves were not making me any cooler. Now that the great moment was approaching I began to wonder whether there could possibly be any chance whatever of success. But I pulled myself together. This was not the moment for wavering.

With mocking slowness the day crept by. All preparations had been made and there was absolutely nothing left to do. I kept thinking of the night, now two years ago, before I had set out for England. Then, too, time had dragged.

A clock struck six. Shortly afterwards we heard the guard coming along with his rattling trolley. The time had come. Cell doors were opening and slamming shut. Suddenly the icy calm of determination descended on me. I saw that my two cell-mates were considerably more nerve-racked than I was. Van der Bor pleaded with me, tears in his eyes. "For God's sake, Pieter, don't go. They'll only shoot you."

By this time, however, my determination was unshakable. Silently I shook hands with my friends, unable to utter a word. I felt that this was goodbye for ever. Through the hole under the wash-basin I exchanged one more word with Ubbink. All O.K. We knew exactly what we were going to do.

Our cell door was flung open, food was pushed in, the door closed. I pulled off my outer garments, and as soon as I heard the trolley turn the corner I gave the signal—one knock on the wall: Now!

I climbed on the bed, drew out the nails, opened the transom and looked out. All clear. A short distance away I saw a shock of fair hair sticking out of a transom above a door: my future companion was also making sure. With the greatest possible speed and silence we each squeezed through the bars. I grazed my shoulder painfully, but a few moments later I was standing in the tiled corridor. My outer clothes and the mattress-rope were handed down to me by my cell-mates, and the window was already closing behind me. My fellow gaolbreaker had worked as fast as I had, and together we raced to the empty cell by the corner. Fortunately the door was still ajar and we scurried into the cell, pushing the door back to its original position. Ubbink and I now had a good look at each other; he was a well-built young man with a pink boyish face. With tense smiles we patted each other encouragingly on the back. Holding our breath, we could hear our hearts beating like kettledrums.

The guard with his trolley took an unconscionable time to come back. At last we heard him; he was whistling *"Mamaschen gib mir ein Pferdchen"*, something on the lines of "Daddy won't give me a bow-wow"—it was excruciating.

Once he had passed the cell in which we were crouching we opened the door and crept after him along the corridor until we came to the lavatory we had selected. In we shot and locked the door behind us. Silence reigned. We had not been heard. Luckily for us, there were three lavatories in a row, which lessened our chance of discovery, for we had to hide in the one we were in for six hours. I sat on the seat, Ubbink on the floor. At rare intervals we talked in whispers. We even smoked an occasional cigarette. Though our nerves had calmed down considerably, we noticed how our hands shook as we passed each other a light.

Once or twice a guard came along to use the lavatory. Twice our door was shaken, and each time one of us, as arranged, shouted *"Besetzt"*—"In use." Suddenly it occurred to me that it would be bad luck if one of the guards had a stomach upset and came more than once, in which case it might strike him as odd that the same lavatory was constantly in use. However, fortunately, our German friends suffered no such upsets.

It became exceedingly hot in that small cubicle. The weather was thundery, and when we glanced out of our small window we could see distant lightning flashing in the sky. At eight o'clock we heard the cell doors being opened again as the prisoners were putting the chairs with their clothes out in the corridor. Would the guards notice that two sets were missing? All went well. Silence fell over the prison, and slowly, irritatingly slowly, darkness closed in. We drew the black-out screen across the lavatory window and lit the light, grinning at each other in the brightness. Somewhere in the building a radio was turned on.

It was exactly a quarter to twelve by Ubbink's watch when the tense silence was broken by a roll of thunder; the wind rose and the rain came down in a deafening downpour. With this utter darkness nature was playing into our hands.

I felt a surge of optimism and whispered, "Shall we risk it?" Ubbink nodded. His round face was pale but fearless. We turned out the light and removed the black-out screen. The prisoner in the next cell must have heard something, for he made an audible movement. In a sudden burst of exuberance I tapped the V-sign on the wall. It was immediately answered.

The rain was still pouring down in torrents. I was sure that in the cells looking our way four pairs of eyes would be trying to pierce the gloom; I was even prepared to wager that they were as excited as we were. We waited until the sentry had played his searchlight along the windows and then immediately looped our makeshift rope round one of the bars. If the bars were wide enough apart to allow us to pass through they would be more help than hindrance. We tied our clothes to the end of the rope and lowered them, and then I squeezed myself through the bars.

Some thirty or forty feet below lay the black earth. I felt the moist roughness of the wall, and the uneven rope cut my fingers as I slid down as fast as I dared. At any moment I might hear the stutter of an automatic pistol. My stockinged feet touched the rain-sodden ground, and I quickly crouched against the foot of the wall. The rain ran down my back, wet and chilly. A few moments later Ubbink came sliding down and we drew the rope after us. Not ten seconds later the searchlight beam came playing across the wall, high above us. Bent double, we slipped over to the shadow of the nearby chapel, where we should be out of sight of the sentries. We threw the rope down a well and hurried into our clothes.

Now we were outside the prison. Two stages had been covered, but the worst was yet to come: the barbed-wire entanglement, distant by some fifty yards of open space. Like Red Indians we crawled along, flat on our stomachs and very slowly. We were within fifteen feet of the wire when we heard footsteps, hobnailed boots coming nearer and nearer: a sentry was approaching. Our faces pressed to the ground, we lay motionless. For one ghastly instant the gleam of his boots flickered before my half-closed eyes, but the man failed to notice us and continued calmly on his round.

After a short wait we crawled on to the barbed-wire entanglement. Ubbink tackled it first, and the noise he made sounded fearfully loud to me. I had so often looked out of my cell window and seen the sentries standing and gazing out over it and then skirting it with clockwork regularity. But now it was pouring with rain and the Germans were no doubt huddled in their sentry-boxes, cursing the downpour and the wind that made the trees creak and rustle. This thunderstorm was very lucky for us.

Suddenly the urgency of the situation swept over me, and before Ubbink was clear of the barbed wire I began to climb over it. My feet found little support on the shifting strands, but with my hands tucked inside my cuffs I plodded on. Hardly had I reached the top before the barbs did their work and held me. I wrenched and, at the cost of some unsightly ragged tears, freed myself.

"Quick, quick!" I whispered, suddenly terrified lest, now that freedom was in sight, we should fail. A few hundred yards and we would reach the ditch. How deep was it? We didn't know. A searchlight flashed on and began to play vaguely over the ground. It was erratic in its course and seemed to jump right over us. Darkness returned and we arrived at the ditch.

Again we took off our shoes and top clothes and then stepped into the water. Our feet sank into the mud, but the water never came higher than our waists and the ditch was no more than fifteen feet wide. We clambered up the opposite bank, through the reeds, and found ourselves on grass. We were free! Beside ourselves with joy, we threw our arms exultantly round each other. But we were aware that, though the worst might be over, our journey's end was not yet in sight.

We set off towards the town of Tilburg, six miles to the south, as fast as we could go. We knew of an address there, given to Ubbink by his former cell-mate, Jan Kist, where we might find help. And now our training proved useful. We knew that escaped prisoners invariably and instinctively try to get as far away from their prison as they can. But when no vehicle is available such an attempt is useless. It is more important to leave no traces, especially as we were certain that before very long the Germans would be in pursuit with police dogs. We walked in circles, therefore, avoiding roads as much as possible. At one point we separated, each covering a large arc before we rejoined each other farther on. We crossed cornfields and jumped over ditches. Sometimes we walked along the middle of a ditch, a good method of throwing dogs off the scent.

Towards morning we reached the outskirts of Tilburg, and we went straight on to the address we had been given. It turned out to be that of a chemist's shop, not a private house, and, though we rang and rang, no one answered the door. That was a serious disappointment, for it meant that we should have to wait until eight o'clock at the earliest for the shop to open, by which time we ought to be in hiding. It was only half-past five, yet there were already a number of people in the streets, and our bedraggled appearance was attracting their attention. I said, "We must manage to get inside somewhere. Our absence may be discovered at any moment now, and it won't be long before a general alarm is sent out."

We made for the centre of the town and walked past a Catholic church. We had no choice. We decided to go in and throw ourselves on the mercy of a priest. He might be prepared to help us. There were very few collaborators among the Dutch clergy. Most prisoners of war who escaped from Germany made straight for the first church tower they saw on Dutch territory. Ninety-nine times out of a hundred they were received with friendship.

We were both Protestants, and we entered the church hesitantly. Mass was being said, people were going in and out, and the building was filled with the low murmur of prayer. We found seats and tried to catch sight of a priest. But we saw none. After a while we realized that even here we were attracting notice; people were turning round and staring at us. At last, however, a sacristan passed near us, and I touched his arm and asked him whether we could have a word with the priest. The sacristan told us to follow him, led us to a small room and requested us to wait there.

The door opened and the priest came in. He raised his eyebrows as he looked us up and down questioningly. I thought the occasion demanded honesty, and I told him the truth. He plainly had his doubts as he listened to our truly fantastic story. Wisely he decided to call someone who knew more about such matters than he. Meanwhile he asked us to go on waiting in that small room.

About an hour later a sturdy figure walked in, a typical Brabant man. He took Ubbink to some other part of the church, and then returned and began to interrogate me scientifically.

"Are you a policeman?" I asked.

He nodded, adding, "But don't let that worry you. Tell me some more."

Again I narrated our adventures. He then left me, no

doubt to interrogate Ubbink. Presently he returned, with Ubbink, and said to us, "I can't say that I can altogether believe your story, but you have given me enough details to make a check. I shall ask London about you, and God help you if you have been telling me lies. And no nonsense, now, for you wouldn't survive ten seconds."

He took us first to his house, and that night, when it was dark, he lent us bicycles and the three of us cycled to a farm near a place called Moergestel. Arrangements had been made with the farmer, who asked no questions but took us straight to an attic. The policeman said, "You are almost on top of the prison here, and the Germans aren't likely to think of looking for you so near."

He promised that he would come back the next day and bade us a curt good-night. We sat down, a little dashed, on a high double bed. Events had been moving rapidly during these last twenty-four hours.

"We've been damned lucky," Ubbink commented, and I agreed with him. In spite of our uncertainty we slept like logs. It was our first night under a free roof for five months.

CHAPTER 13

ROBBERY WITH VIOLENCE

THE MAN from Tilburg turned out to be a former police inspector named Van Bilsen. He had resigned because of his objections to the Nazis and was now porter in a factory. He was a powerfully built man who did not seem to know fear. When he entered our attic next day he was considerably friendlier than he had been the day before. He was far less suspicious, and he told us that our escape had caused a major upheaval in the district. The S.D. had barricaded all roads and were combing the fields with teams of dogs. Whole districts of Tilburg and 's Hertogenbosch were being searched.

"It looks as if we have passed our examination," Ubbink remarked with a wry smile when Van Bilsen had departed. He had told us to stay where we were for a while, until the chase had died down a little. Meanwhile he would establish contact with England and ask for instructions.

We had to wait a long time. The Germans were tenacious and left little undone. Meanwhile we were peacefully, if impatiently, waiting amidst the old-fashioned mahogany furniture, within a quarter of an hour's walk of the prison, smoking cigarettes and reading Nazified newspapers. At night we were occasionally able to stroll in the garden among the dahlias for a breath of fresh air. It was too dangerous to do so during the day.

One day Van Bilsen arrived and took a piece of paper from his pocket. "Take a look at this," he said. We did, and it infuriated us.

REWARD

500 Guilders

Two men
JOHAN BERNHARD UBBINK
born 22.5.21. at Doesberg

last known domicile at Arnhem
officer in the mercantile marine
and
PIETER DOURLEIN
born 2.2.18 at Veere

last known domicile at Amsterdam
bricklayer

are wanted by the Criminal Investigation Department

for

ROBBERY WITH VIOLENCE

Anyone able to assist the police in their investigation, please communicate with their local police station.

"What's all this nonsense?" I asked.

"It's the wording of an appeal shown on the screen at all cinemas," Van Bilsen replied, "together with your photographs."

"Robbery with violence," Ubbink exclaimed. "Just what the scum would think up."

"It makes it very clear that they are eager for your company," was Van Bilsen's opinion. "They must be worried."

"I should have thought we were worth more than £50," I said. "I'll send them a note."

I got pen and paper and wrote a long letter to the S.D. officer at 's Hertogenbosch, telling him what I thought of a police force that had sunk to such depths in the service of an enemy. I added that I was no more a highway robber than I was a bricklayer, and I ended by saying that by the time he received this I should be safely back in England. I also explained that our friends in Haaren Prison had nothing to do with our escape and should not be held responsible. That same night a courier took the letter to the north of the country, where it would be posted. I had enjoyed writing that letter.

After two weeks in that attic Van Bilsen thought the day had come to make a move. German vigilance was relaxing and it was not advisable to stay too long in the same place. One dark night he came to fetch us. We said goodbye to the taciturn farmer—we had seen scarcely another soul—thanked him for his help and nourishing hospitality, and entered a closed car that stood waiting. A stranger was sitting at the wheel. We felt a little uneasy, but Van Bilsen told us not to worry. We drove along, at great speed, towards Tilburg; about halfway there a red light was waved in the roadway in front of us. Van Bilsen swore and put his hand in his hip-pocket. In the dimmed lights of the headlamps we could see several men in uniform. The driver reduced speed as if he were about to stop, then, when he was almost on top of them, stepped on the gas. In sudden alarm, the men scattered to the side of the road. It was all over in a few seconds. The car raced by and had soon turned a corner.

Not a word was said. In Tilburg we got out in silence; the car drove off straight away and we turned into a dark and narrow alley. After we had gone some yards we were told to wait a few moments. Van Bilsen returned with a man whom he introduced to us as Vinken, then hastily departed.

Vinken silently led the way through the black-out. It was all very mysterious. An hour later we were comfortably drinking imitation coffee in a pleasant living-room in a house on Pius Square in the very centre of the town, as the guests of Mr. and Mrs. Lauwerrijssens, who had agreed to put us up for a while. Their living quarters were over a busy baker's shop, and during the daytime we should have to hide in a small room upstairs.

Was it not dangerous, we asked, after we had been introduced to our hosts. They shrugged their shoulders. Things had changed a lot in Holland since we had left the country. Everybody was hiding and helping people to hide. The Jews, who had lived mainly in the big towns, were now scattered all over the country. Thousands of young men who refused to go to Germany had vanished from their homes and were lying low in the houses of people they had never seen before but who were ready to help. Of course there was some danger, but there were not enough Germans to search house after house. Occasionally they raided some houses, but usually the Nazi police waited for a tip from an informer. For helping Jews the penalty was eight months to a year in prison. For aiding people who refused to go to Germany you were not even arrested unless you were unlucky. "What do they do with people who help enemy agents to escape?" I asked. "It hardly bears telling," Mr. Lauwerrijssens said, and husband and wife smiled.

How long, we wondered, was all this going to last?

The days crept by. And though the Lauwerrijssens were charming people we were sharply aware that our presence put them in considerable danger. This was not what we had risked our lives for; we had escaped to get away, not to lurk in attics. Our tempers began to fray, and it was a welcome relief when our host came up in the evening to listen to the radio he took from its hiding-place and to experiment with anti-jamming devices.

We determined that contact must be made with England. Already during our stay at the farm we had drawn up a message announcing our escape and asking for help to enable us to get out of the country as soon as possible. We knew that Van Bilsen and Vinken had got this message through to Belgium, whence it had been sent to London. We were still awaiting the answer.

Slowly we began to realize the great damage done by the Germans to the communications with England. Actually agents were no longer being dropped into German hands, and another service in England had already sent a few men who were working freely in Holland, getting daily messages through to their head-quarters. But we did not know about this. Our messages had to be taken to Switzerland by a long and dangerous route. All this made us more determined to return to London as soon as possible. Meanwhile we were discussing a scheme with Van Bilsen to form a new organization with which we could make contact immediately upon our return to London. We were trying to work out a plan to make an attack on the Haaren prison and liberate our colleagues.

After a few more weeks our inspector came to tell us that an answer had come from England. It was not particularly helpful. Would we do what we could to reach England, or at any rate to get to a neutral country where we could be given help.

This message was a shock to us. "They might as well have told us to go and sit out on the roof," I said. "I could have thought that one up myself."

"I imagine they are a bit suspicious of the whole business," Ubbink said. "But it hardly seems possible to believe that they still haven't caught on to the fact that their radio links are in German hands. Are they still talking to the Germans, thinking they are in touch with their own people?"

"In that case," I speculated, "the Germans will have sent them some fearful lies about us. Perhaps they'll even say we've gone over to the other side." This was a great joke, and we laughed heartily. Nevertheless we were sadly puzzled.

As a matter of fact that was exactly what had happened. After our escape the Germans had warned London that we were working for the enemy. It has never become quite clear to us whether the British authorities believed this. Probably they did not know what to think and decided to take the most prudent course. They could have sent a boat or a plane to pick us up, but might not the Germans be waiting for it? These things did not occur to us at the moment when we were endangering the lives of good people and when we thought that the news of our escape would be received with enthusiastic approval.

That something had to be done was clear. We could not stay where we were, and we decided to try and make for Switzerland. Could Van Bilsen procure us some identity papers? He promised to try. But as we had spent six weeks with the Lauwerrijssens it was time for us to move on again. We spent another ten days in some other attic, after which Van Bilsen took us to his own place, for now that we were about to leave it was simpler if we were at hand. He could get us papers only with considerable difficulty; and not only that, for a long journey we should need money. And that was even harder. The solution was offered by Ubbink's brother, who knew a way of transferring money to a Paris bank where we could collect it.

At last everything was ready. We were under no illusions. We knew that we would have to face hardship and danger in many forms.

CHAPTER 14

THE PARIS EXPRESS

THE MORNING of November 11th, 1943, was chilly, dark and unfriendly—not a day to cause us to feel regret at leaving our fatherland. Even so, it wasn't going to be for long.

It was still very early, though there were already a number of factory workers in the streets, but they were too self-centred to pay much attention to the three of us. It had been agreed that Van Bilsen would take us to Antwerp, after which we would have to find our own way. We had been given two addresses, one in Paris and one at Maîche on the Swiss border. Our false passports would be of no use at the frontiers; they were good enough for hotels, but not for close examination.

On the outskirts of Tilburg a car was waiting. Van Bilsen spoke a few words to the driver and off we went. If only everything went as smoothly as this! At great speed we made for Baarle-Nassau, the Belgian enclave near the border. We passed occasional German patrols, but they paid no attention to us, and Van Bilsen's confidence communicated itself to us. I stared out at the dark, untilled fields and thought how little I had been able to do for my country during these last eight months. But it wouldn't be long now.

It had not yet struck seven and it was still hardly light when the car stopped in a quiet country lane with not a soul in sight.

"From here we go on foot, boys," Van Bilsen said.

It wasn't his first trip, that was obvious. We said goodbye to the driver of the car, who drove off at remarkable speed. I shivered. The car took with it our illusion of protection as well as its pleasant warmth. In the chill loneliness of dawn we felt considerably less sure of ourselves.

Silently we plodded ahead and after a quarter of an hour arrived at a small farm, where we came to a halt. Van Bilsen went in and returned with two policemen in uniform, startling us for a moment. The men's demeanour, however, showed everything was in order and we solemnly shook hands, grinning a little at our alarm.

We moved off, a curious little procession; sometimes we went straight across the fields, sometimes in a semicircle to avoid certain farms. Not a word was spoken, for we were in the frontier area. In ten minutes' time we should be in Belgium.

Ubbink and I were wondering what would happen next, when the two policemen stopped. One of them said, "You're in Belgium now, and this is where we must go back. Follow this little road. The first house you come to will be a little café where you can wait for the bus to Turnhout. I think it goes at eight."

We said goodbye, the policemen gave us a formal salute, and turned on their heels.

The café was very Belgian, its façade covered with all kinds of enamelled advertisements inviting one to partake of a variety of drinks or to become a member of some insurance society or another. The proprietor was pottering about in trousers and singlet, and having supplied us with cups of imitation coffee he went on with sweeping the floor, leaving us to our own devices. By eight o'clock there were quite a few workmen, all waiting for the bus, which arrived at a quarter-past eight. Van Bilsen bought the tickets, for his Brabant accent was the least likely to be noticed as unusual. The bus went to Turnhout via Poppel, and at Turnhout we took a tram to Antwerp.

It was still fairly early when we arrived at the city, which was only just waking up and looked unexpectedly unwashed and hungry. It was by no means the gay old Antwerp I had known in the past. But this was hardly the time to be looking around, and we went straight to the Central Station to board a train which was soon to leave for Brussels. Van Bilsen handed us two optimistic single tickets for Mons and we parted, with a firm handclasp, from the man who had helped us so long and so efficiently.

The journey to Brussels was uneventful. We pretended to sleep, which, considering the time of day, was not difficult. In Brussels we had to wait for a couple of hours and drank a glass of beer at the station buffet. Though there were plenty of German military about, no check was made.

Some time during the afternoon we arrived at Mons. Again the journey had been straightforward, but from snatches of overheard conversation we gathered that crossing the frontier was not going to be child's play. There was said to be a very strict control on both the Belgian and French sides, and a sharp look-out was being kept on the stations near the frontier for people who were trying to cross on foot.

We stood on the cobbles outside Mons station, wondering what would be our best plan. The town was grey and unfriendly, and we had no contacts. Nor did we know the way. We would have to find someone to take us across.

Our previous success made us think of a priest; that would probably be the safest way of getting information and help. We walked about until we found a church. We rang the bell of the priest's house and the door was opened by a woman. We asked for *monsieur le curé* and were admitted into the hall.

A small, rotund priest appeared, all smiles. He looked friendly enough, but unfortunately he spoke only French, a language of which I knew nothing and Ubbink very little. Ubbink did his utmost to make the priest understand; but, whether he did or not, we soon realized that we were making no headway, and with many smiles we were conducted to the door and found ourselves outside on the pavement once more.

What next? It would not be advisable to wander round town too long. A hotel? We could try, but we should still have the same problem tomorrow. And there were many churches in Mons; surely we could find one priest who knew some Flemish. We were lucky. We happened to pass a monastery, and I thought to myself, "Odd if there weren't a Flemish monk." Again we rang a bell, and again we were admitted.

"Hollandais," we said to the man who opened the postern. He nodded and went away, to return with a monk who addressed us in Flemish.

"Please come with me," he said.

We followed him to a small room containing a large crucifix and some green plush chairs and immediately told him our story—not all of it, but not a word that was not true. The monk listened without moving a muscle. At the end he spoke. "That's a fine story. Don't you know that all parachutists have to be handed over to the authorities? How dare you come here? I do not wish to harbour you."

Flemish is a very homely language, but he made it sound quite the contrary. I stood up and stepped over to him. "Please realize that we are not going to allow ourselves to be taken alive. So, are you going to let us out or are we going to have to make sure of a safe exit?"

The monk was thinking hard. "You tell me you came by Poppel this morning. Did anything strike you there—anything of a temporary nature, but very obvious? If you can answer that question satisfactorily I am prepared to reconsider your story."

In amazement we stared at him. What could he mean? It was clearly a test of some sort. Had we seen anything out-of-the-way at Poppel? The monk's expression was not unfriendly—anything out of the usual at Poppel?

"Well," I said, "all I can remember is that the road was up and we had to make a fairly wide detour, but———"

The Capuchin's solemn face showed obvious relief. A weight had been lifted off his mind. Suddenly he was all smiles and became almost jovial. "Sit down, gentlemen. I am entirely at your service. I can tell that you were speaking the truth. I, too, came by Poppel this morning, so I know now that you did, as you said. You must forgive my hesitation, but there are so many unreliable people about these days. Last week they shot three of our patriots for being involved in something similar."

The monk took us to a small hotel which he assured us would be safe. He also gave us the address of a place near the frontier. We were to go there the following day, and, with God's help, we would succeed in our enterprise.

We had an excellent meal and went to sleep comparatively happy. The next morning we walked to the address given us, a small house on the edge of a mining village. We knocked at the door and a woman opened it. She responded to our broken French with a hearty welcome in Dutch, "Come in, boys. Consider yourselves at home." She was of Dutch origin, a widow with seven children. We were touched by her hospitality, for it was obvious that she was not well-to-do. Nothing was too good for us; she pressed all kinds of rationed food on us and would not hear of payment. "The fewer people who know, the better."

When darkness had fallen we set off through the back door along a track that could hardly be called a path. The widow wore a shawl over her head and strode along in large hobnailed boots. We walked for about half an hour, then suddenly turned into a little house; the kitchen-living room was full of people who eyed us curiously as we stood blinking in the unaccustomed bright light. Our guide spoke a few words to a small man with a moustache, then turned to us and said, "It's all arranged. These kind people will help you. Have a good journey, boys!" Giving us each a motherly hug and kiss, she departed into the night with a cheerful "Bonne nuit".

So we were in France. For it was France, and the warmth of the room and the friendliness of the people enveloped us. It was curious—the number of good-hearted people we were meeting; goodness and friendliness that knew no frontiers. Smiling, they gave help that might well cost them their lives. "Any man who is against the Boche is a friend of ours", that was their slogan. Against such a spirit we felt that the New Order could not prevail.

The master of the house, the man with the moustache, spoke a few words of Flemish, and we talked as much as we could, eking out our vocabularies with gestures.

Bottles of wine were produced and glasses were kept filled. We were told the latest war news. The Germans were getting some bad knocks in Russia. Had we heard that Kiev had been retaken? Our host produced a small, antiquated school atlas from a kitchen drawer and laboriously, with a black-nailed finger, found Kiev and traced an imaginary line across the country—the front line. "Ici," he exclaimed, "Boche Kaputt."

After some more rummaging he produced his Croix de Guerre, gained during the First World War, and gave us to understand that he was only too pleased to have a chance to do something for the Allied cause in this one. The wine flowed. One of the black-haired, pleasant-looking daughters gave a highly successful rendering of one of Lucienne Boyer's songs. Life had not been so pleasant for a very long time.

We were woken up early next morning and life was considerably less pleasant. We felt awful. Our knees were sagging and our temples hammering. With deep sighs we ate a breakfast of thick slices of war-time bread. There was a drizzle, and the drone of aeroplanes reminded us that there was still a war on and that we were about to undertake a long and perilous trek across strange country. Our first port of call was to be Paris.

How to get there was the question. Our host gave us a knowing smile. He was a railway man and worked in the frontier station of Feignies. He was going to see to it that we boarded the train without being worried by the German station guards.

An hour after he had left for work Ubbink and I set out, accompanied by his wife. We walked straight to the station, where we were taken into the stationmaster's office. The train was standing ready to leave, the travellers were all in their places. Our host of the night before came along and pushed two tickets into our hands and took our small case.

"Look sharp. The moment the train starts, you run that way. I shall keep a door open and you jump in. Nobody will notice. It's the best method. It has never failed yet." Nor did it fail this time. Five minutes later we were safely aboard the Paris express.

It was a long journey, and the chance of being caught appeared greater in France than it had in Belgium. We had been warned against French collaborators, dangerous people, and as there was no possibility of us passing ourselves off as natives we would have to give our journey an apparent necessity. We therefore followed a method which, at first thought, seemed terrifying, but which in actual fact was almost fool-proof. We sought a compartment containing several Germans in uniform, settled in and struck up conversations all round. We volunteered the information that we were Dutch workers who had offered to work on an airfield near Marseilles. It was a good method and we kept to it for the whole of our journey through France. It had another advantage: whenever the French police checked the papers of the people on the train, we were almost certain to be left alone, as we were so obviously friends of the German military.

Late that afternoon we entered Paris. It was no longer raining, and under the grey sky the town looked impressive and not inhospitable. We left the Gare du Nord and began our search for the Rue de La Fayette and the small hotel that had been recommended to us in Mons, the proprietor being a Fleming. Without much difficulty we found the place and asked for a room. The hotelier, looking exceedingly bad-tempered, inspected our passports, raised his eyebrows, and threw down the two blank forms he had already taken from a drawer.

"So you're Dutch, eh?" he commented as he rose to his feet.

In silence he led us up a narrow stairway, the carpet getting thinner and more worn the higher we went, the paint progressively shabbier. The proprietor opened the door of an attic and pointed at the window and the fire-escape with a meaning look before he left us with a curt good-night. All his gruffness was a blind: here was yet another of those good people who were prepared to take risks for complete strangers. Surely, we thought, our good luck could not hold unbroken.

We decided to minimize our own risks and stay indoors as much as possible, but a visit to the Banque de France to see whether the money sent by Ubbink's brother had arrived was necessary. We had only a few hundred francs left when we reached Paris, and those went straight away on a simple meal. But when we got to the bank we found that nothing had been heard of the money. We left the enormous building, walking uneasily past the gendarmes who, armed to the teeth, were zealously guarding Pétain's filthy lucre.

By way of the Tuileries, we went to the other bank of the river, looking for the Rue de Sèvres and a monastery where we were to ask for Father Lauwerrijssens, a relative of our Tilburg hosts. Here we had our first disappointment. We were informed that the monk had gone on a journey—they did not add that he was on his way to England. So there we were without money and without any idea what to do.

Every day we called at the bank, and every day the cashier shook his head. It could not go on long like that.

Hunger was beginning to gnaw and the hotel bill was piling up. Our room was unheated and, as the rain had set in again, Paris was becoming increasingly inimical.

I thought of a plan: not a noble plan, but an adequate one. Let us knock down some German, preferably an officer, rob him of his money and papers and run. "After all," I said, "we have already been accused of robbery with violence."

In our room there was a heavy brass candlestick. I reduced it to its essentials and made it an effective weapon. We would have one more try at collecting our money from the bank, and if we were still unsuccessful we would post ourselves at some quiet, dark spot and choose a suitable victim.

Our stomachs rattling, we set out in the drizzle. The candlestick weighed heavy in my pocket. We entered the Banque de France, and I sat down on a marble bench while Ubbink went to the paying-out desk. The cashier knew him by sight now, so that my hopes rose when he stayed away longer than usual. When he returned his face was alight with relief.

"O.K.!" he said, waving notes at me. I, too, sighed with relief. I had not relished the prospect of turning into a cosh-boy.

With a marked unanimity of purpose we set out to look for a place in which to eat a substantial but not too expensive meal without having to hand over food coupons we had not got. We found such a place in Montmartre and life was rosy again. We were a little over-excited and very exuberant, and forthwith ordered a bottle of wine, even though it cost as much as ten peace-time bottles. Next we went to a *café chantant* where they served honest pre-war cognac and where our solitude was immediately alleviated by a couple of charming Parisiennes in rustling transparent gowns. We had to leave, however—not that we were averse to female company, but because too many Germans were coming in for our comfort, especially as many of them wore S.S. and S.D. uniforms. And the nicest girls in Paris were not worth the risk we should have been running had we stayed.

CHAPTER 15

THE SAFEST ROUTE

THOUGH the evening had reconciled us to Paris, we did not regret having the means to proceed on our route. We paid the hotel bill, said goodbye to the considerate proprietor and left carrying a suitcase and a parcel of black-market rolls and fragrant sausage. Our next destination was Maîche, and from that village we hoped to be able to enter Switzerland. Maîche was not on the railway, but, according to the map, Belfort, which was not far away, was.

In the early morning we arrived at the Gare de l'Est and climbed into a high, old-fashioned carriage, choosing, in the absence of German soldiery, an empty compartment and settling down to apparent sleep. But we were far from sleepy. The journey we were setting out on was risky, especially as we had no idea of what forms danger might take so that we could not prepare ourselves for them in advance.

It was a seemingly endless, monotonous journey. Our compartment was soon overcrowded and everyone was uncomfortable and bad-tempered. Germans occasionally entered the compartment as travellers, not to check papers. Even so, we got into conversation with them, and in so doing elaborated our cover-story that we were Dutch labourers on our way to work on some fortifications near the border. Marseilles had had to be shifted somewhat.

To our surprise, not a single check was made during our eight-hour journey, though we saw French gendarmes and German military policemen at every station. They did not, however, interfere with the people in the train. The landscape we were passing through was gently undulating and almost grey in colour, but gradually we came to higher country; slopes were steepening and we could see endless rows of gnarled vines as far as the eye could reach. On our left were the mountains, some snow-capped. In that direction lay Switzerland.

Seat-conscious, but in cheerful spirits because of our luck so far, we got out of the train that afternoon at Belfort. We were already discussing the possibilities of a good hot meal and of the road transport to Maîche when suddenly Ubbink seized my arm and halted me. He had observed a group of German M.P.s by the exit carefully checking papers. We turned in the opposite direction and after scrutinizing the platform and its exits made a few cautious enquiries. We learned that Belfort was the centre of a prohibited area and that the Germans were having trouble with the maquis and its smuggling activities. The prohibited area ran parallel with the Swiss frontier deep into France.

We hung about the platform, hoping for a train going the other way to take us out of this trap. The only change in the situation was that a German started walking up and down the platform, eyeing us suspiciously. At that moment I caught sight of the goods department, and it occurred to me that such places invariably communicate with the street. Now or never, I thought. I took hold of a trolley that was standing near, and Ubbink, quick on the uptake, stooped down and dragged a heavy box on to it. With the box and our own case we entered the goods shed. A French official immediately came over to us. I put a finger to my lips—an international gesture—and without saying a word the man stood aside and let us pass.

Five seconds later we were out in the street; crossing the station yard, we zigzagged along some narrow alleys. Nobody was following us. In a small restaurant we recovered from our narrow escape over plates of fried liver and chips. It took us some time to plan the next move. The best route was by bus—the cake-tin buses that still sway round the French countryside as did the old stage-coaches. We went, and found it to be a lengthy trip through steep, mountainous country. The other passengers studied us the whole time, eyeing us from head to foot, but no one said a word.

Towards nightfall we arrived at Maîche. The little village was already asleep, and after a good deal of foot-slogging we came across a man who put us on the right road. The address we had been given was that of a Dutch family, who received us with open arms. We were given food and sleeping accommodation, and the eldest son told us, "Tomorrow I shall arrange for your trip across. Now you must sleep, for you are in for a strenuous and sleepless time."

We asked him what he thought our chances were. "Excellent," he said, "and if the Germans do become troublesome we'll shoot our way through. We have never failed yet. They are scared to death of the French maquis."

It was fairly late in the morning when the mistress of the house called us and brought us our breakfast in bed: real fragrant tea and fresh, curly rolls with ham and marmalade—a good start to the day. For the first time for days the sun came out and we could see it shining on

[151]

the snowy mountain-tops. The healthy, invigorating mountain air came in through the open windows: this wouldn't be a bad place to stay, I reflected, far away from all that wretched espionage business. I ought to join the maquis. Here war could be without treachery, without torture, a war in which the people were spontaneously fighting the invader.

Yet I knew only too well how fleeting such thoughts were. I had to go on. My companion and I had to cross the border, not just to save ourselves but to try to bring to an end one of the most horrible tragedies of the war. There were our comrades at Haaren, and if possible they must be liberated before the Germans turned over the last page of that particular story.

That afternoon the eldest son took us to a farm near the border, the rallying point for the expedition that was to be made that night. He pointed to a mountain-top high above us. "That's Switzerland," he said, "and your liberty."

Upon our arrival the farmer greeted us with, "Better go and lie down. We meet tonight at ten o'clock, and you'll need all the rest you can get."

The way everyone was talking, it sounded as if a terrible ordeal was looming before us. We stretched ourselves out on some straw and dozed. When we woke up there were already several new faces round us. As evening drew on, more and more men arrived, all carrying large sacks.

"What are those?" I asked.

"Contraband," we were told. "We exchange this stuff for arms. And you'll have to do your bit."

About twenty of us were ready by now; most of the men drank one or two large beakers of wine, and as they sat there on the straw, on the bare boards, or on low stools round a rough wooden table, they looked like a scene

from a Wild West film. Nor were arms lacking. Several
of the men had sub-machine guns of German or British
manufacture on their knees; they were to form the van-
guard and the rear of our small convoy.

Before we set out it was made clear to us that we would
have to keep up with the others. If we failed to do so it
would be just too bad; we should have to be left behind,
for Switzerland had to be reached by daybreak to avoid
discovery.

We set out between ten and eleven, in single file along
narrow, slippery mountain tracks. Not only were there
armed men in front and at the rear but also guarding
our flanks. At first we went down into the valley towards the river which formed the frontier line. After about
an hour the leader gave a sign that henceforth the strictest
silence must be observed, for we were nearing the
imaginary line between France and Switzerland. My
Dutch companion and I were beginning to realize that
our laden rucksacks were not as light as we had first
thought them to be.

Suddenly we slowed up. The humming of a powerful
engine could be heard, coming up from the ground,
rapidly increasing in volume and reverberating among
the hills. Our companions drew us off the path, and we
all crouched behind rocks as we saw a feeble searchlight
playing over the ground and across the landscape, picking
out objects here and there. It was an armoured car
patrolling, and after a while the steel-clad vehicle rumbled
past, its crew unaware of our presence. The men lowered
their guns and stood up again.

Now we began to run, across the valley, across a road.
We took off our shoes and socks and rolled up our trouser-
legs to wade across the river, after which we followed a
meandering and steadily ascending mountain-path.

Though we were now on Swiss territory, we were by no means safe, for the Swiss customs men, if they caught us, would ruthlessly take us back to the frontier. Rest was out of the question. And we had a four-hours march ahead, upward and largely over snow-covered ground. An hour after we had crossed the frontier I had reached the end of my endurance and began to stagger. Silently one of the Frenchmen took my pack, flung it on top of his own and made it possible for me to stumble along after him. By encouraging Ubbink I was encouraging myself. My whole body seemed to be wrenched to pieces by this breathless climb. At length sensation and pain ceased, except in our feet, which at one moment seemed lumps of ice and the next red-hot coals.

As dawn broke a sudden halt was called. Where were we? We were there. We had arrived. Rucksacks were thrown off and crashed down on the rocks. The French sat down, lit their Gauloises and gave us congratulatory pats on the back.

Ten minutes' rest. Then we had to get to our feet again and say goodbye to the men of the maquis, except for one who was going to see us on our way. He took us along a fairly level road lined with fir trees. There was not a soul in sight. After about an hour we came to a compound of simple barracks made of tarred tree-trunks and encircled by a plain fencing. It was an internment camp.

Our guide asked us to wait and went in. A few moments later he came back with a fair young man in shorts who greeted us in perfect Dutch and welcomed us to Switzerland.

"Will you come with me?" He took us to a small building, and there we collapsed on to chairs. The Frenchman said goodbye without wasting words, and left.

"He is going back tonight," the young man explained. "How they do it is beyond me."

Soon a plain but welcome meal was set before us, and we were asked what help we needed. We told our host that we were Dutch airmen who had been shot down a week or so ago and that we hoped to get to Berne to report to the Netherlands Embassy. We did not think it wise to tell our true story to a perfect stranger, though he was a fellow-countryman. He gave us all the help we wanted—Swiss money to buy railway tickets, and he saw us to our train.

We were still suffering from exhaustion when we got to Berne that night. In the station restaurant we had three cups of black coffee each and, a little refreshed, set out to find the British Embassy. Arrived there, we asked to see the Intelligence Officer. The man immediately placed his services at our disposal, listened to our story, and declared, "You have done splendid work. I shall communicate with London tonight." He patted us on the back and, seeing how tired we were, had us driven by car to a hotel.

"Well, Benny," I said with a sigh of relief, "that's that. We've succeeded at last."

We sank down on our beds, unable to stir another inch. And yet we could not sleep. We lay staring at the ceiling and listening to the rattle of the trams and the other sounds of a city where life seemed normal and there was no black-out.

We guessed we would not be asked to rest on our laurels until the end of the war; but we were safe, and London must by now have received our warning. I fell asleep at last with the thought, "I wish my friends at Haaren knew where we were. It would certainly put their minds at rest."

The following morning we were taken to see the Dutch military attaché, General Van Tricht, who gave us a hearty welcome.

"Thank God!" he exclaimed. "Some facts at last. We knew something had gone wrong, but couldn't see just what it was."

A few days before he had received a message from some Dutch underground group. It announced that we had escaped from prison some weeks previously and according to our colleagues in Haaren we could be trusted.

Everything had to be told and retold down to the smallest detail, and a long telegram was drawn up and despatched to London. It contained all the essential facts, the story of our reception in Holland, that the Germans knew everything about the organization, including all contact addresses in Holland and Switzerland. General van Tricht believed our story, but he wanted to make sure that we were the persons we claimed to be and he sent a very accurate description. "I can send them to Spain along the ordinary route. Do you agree with this, or does the British Service want to give them new instructions?" he asked.

We waited in some suspense. We wanted to go to England because we felt sure that there were many things we could tell the authorities. We also wished to persuade them to liberate the agents we had left behind in prison. We were not very keen on being sent back to Holland before seeing our chiefs. We did not have to wait long. The next morning London responded. The escaped agents were to make their way to England by a safe route. The Swiss authorities told us we must leave the country within a week, or else they would have to intern us.

To England by a safe route? Easier said than done. Which route was safe? We knew of but one route: via the South of France, the Pyrenees, Spain and Gibraltar, but even that was not particularly safe.

General Van Tricht declared, "You have five days in which to recuperate your strength. That will give you time to make arrangements. I shall see to it that you get new clothes and suitable equipment for your journey."

This was no superfluous luxury. The only things we retained were our lounge suits, properly mended, for new clothes might have been a little noticeable in wartime France.

The end of our short spell of freedom soon arrived. We were told to report at a certain address in Geneva, where we would be given our final instructions. Everything seemed well organized. We were handed excellent identity papers, describing us as workers in the Todt Organization, a pocket compass, and the names of a whole string of contact-men. That same night we left by car.

At the frontier we got out, and a Swiss customs official helped us through barbed wire while his colleague kept his German counterpart talking. It was all done inside ten minutes. We were in France again and on our way to yet another frontier.

We avoided farms and main roads. At a small village we took a bus to Grenoble, where we met our first contact in a café opposite the cathedral. The watchword was passed and everything went smoothly. We could tell we were dealing with experienced men. At ten o'clock we were taken to the train that would carry us to Toulouse via Lyon.

On this long cross-country railway journey we followed our well-tried tactics of seeking the company of German soldiers. Again it spared us many an enquiry. At Lyon the French police made a very thorough inspection of identity papers, but Ubbink and I, as friends of Germans, were passed over.

After twelve hours we arrived at Toulouse, where we found our next contact without delay. We had to go to a villa in its own grounds on the outskirts of the town. It was a large place, and there we found some eight or ten men of various nationalities, all waiting to be taken across the Pyrenees into Spain. One man in a beret and with an obviously military bearing took us aside and gave us some details about the situation. The trip across the mountains was dangerous, slow and exhausting; hence he was arranging an alternative method: we were to be transported in packing-cases on a freight train. We felt a certain relief. Our previous expedition in the Alps had not made us any the fonder of mountains.

Some two hours later, as our very mixed company was peacefully sitting down to a meal, there was an alarm. The man in the beret rushed into the room, saying that a raid could be expected any moment. Two men in packing-cases had been found at the frontier and had given way under interrogation. That meant that we had better set out that very night.

We did not even have time to provide ourselves with proper food. Quickly we snatched up what we could and put it into our rucksacks. We left the villa from the back and were taken to the station in small groups. A local train took us to the foot of the mountains. The weather was not bad: dry and not too cold. We climbed a path and found ourselves at the rendezvous. We were struck by the difficulty of the terrain—and we had hardly started yet. I raised my eyes to the walls of rock ahead, to the enormous snow-capped peaks that stood glistening, unapproachable, in the evening light. It would have been a grand spectacle for anyone who liked it.

[158]

An hour's walk brought us to a sheepfold where some sixteen men were already awaiting us. This was the convoy in its entirety, ready to venture on the trip to "free" Spain.

There were two guides, tough, sunburnt young men. One of them made a short speech in which he told us that we were faced by the mountains at their widest and highest, but that, taking everything into consideration, this was the safest route. We must obey instructions unquestioningly, for should we be spotted by a German ski-patrol we would be irrevocably lost. And he added that the group counted above the individual: if one fell behind he would have to be left, maybe to starve.

That was that. At any rate we knew where we were. And we knew that it wasn't going to be a picnic.

We started without much delay. Before long we had left the road and were going along what may have been paths to the initiated. They were slippery and we kept on falling, for few of the company were practised mountaineers. We had set out at a brisk pace, but before very long it had to be slackened. It began to rain, and soon we were soaked through. And of course the rain made the ground even more slippery.

That night was wretched. We stumbled, slid, fell and crawled, and when dawn came we were beginning to shiver. We were putting our feet down as if we had only just learned to walk, for our co-ordination was weakening. As morning dawned, the rain ceased. We soon came to the first snow, and the high peaks surrounding us were ringed with mist. A glance behind us, at the valley of Gascogne, was depressing, for the nearness of the valley, with its veils of rain, clearly showed us how small our progress had been, in spite of our night's arduous toil.

When we came to a mountain hut beside a haystack we

were allowed to rest, but we were not allowed to light a
fire, for the smoke would have betrayed our presence. We
sat still and felt colder than ever. We also felt wretched.
A couple of young lads were beginning to declare that
they could never make it and might as well go back, but
we talked them into having another try.

Our rest lasted a few hours, and I even managed to
sleep for a while, to my own astonishment. And then on
we went again, onward and upward. The layer of snow
grew thicker. I am convinced that nature must have been
most impressive, but I had reached the stage when I no
longer raised my eyes from the ground. Night came and
still we walked, endlessly ascending. Often the snow
came up to our knees; we were wading through it, and
below the snow lay all kinds of man-traps; it was never
possible to get into any kind of regular stride or swing.

Towards morning we came upon another hut. By now
my feet were swollen. We all collapsed on the floor—and
slept. The first few hundred yards that we walked after
that rest were inhuman. Every one of us thought: It's
no good, I can't do it. The young boys began to lag behind. Some of the Frenchmen had done the trip before
and had greater powers of endurance. They would go to
the lads, help them up, support them a little, and carry
their rucksacks. Those mountaineers were towers of
strength. But by now not a man was walking properly.
We were all stumbling and staggering.

By the time darkness fell again we had reached our
limit. In a somewhat sheltered place, free of snow, we
collapsed for the night. Most of us lay where we had been
standing. With the morning light we had to get up.
Though stiff all over, we were somewhat rested. Ubbink
and I had practically no food left, and we could not very
well beg from the others—they had little enough.

Fortunately, Ubbink had, during the last rush, grabbed a bag of lumps of sugar. They were a godsend.

In the afternoon we halted at a mountain stream, but few of us felt like washing. The guides pointed to a distant peak. That was Spain. We were almost beyond caring. With the onset of night we were going down to lower ground, into a valley with a fairly wide river. We had to reach the other side, but there was only one bridge, and that bridge was guarded by a German frontier post. As soon as the patrol had passed, therefore, we were to rush across the bridge and up the other side. There were some awkward moments, but we got across. The next thing was to look out for ski-patrols. Strangely enough, these more concrete dangers called forth our latent energy. We could see that our guides had not been talking idly, for we passed six crosses in a row, the graves of fugitives who had been shot down a few weeks before, an hour or so from safety.

According to our guides, we should reach the border by midday. We were now quickening our pace. We didn't know where we got the strength from, and we didn't stop to wonder. Yet by this time we had been going for four days at a stretch.

The guide proved right. On December 1st, 1943, on the stroke of twelve, we passed the frontier post. Below us, in a valley, we could see a village of small houses clustering round an enormous church.

CHAPTER 16

APPEARANCES AGAINST US

THERE was also a barn in that Spanish frontier village which had been arranged for the reception of refugees from France. I dropped down on the hay. Did I care that I had been told not to leave the place without permission? The villagers were coming, bringing us bread and meat and fruit, and we threw ourselves on the food like hungry wolves.

When I wrenched off my shoes I found that my socks were caked with blood and could hardly be detached from my feet. A young Spanish woman saw this and, telling me to wait a moment, came back with a bowl of water in which to soak my feet and clean them. They were a mass of blisters and raw flesh. She gently bandaged them and gracefully accepted a kiss—the only payment I could make.

Hardly had we eaten before we fell into a deep sleep; and we snored in unison until well into the next day, when we were woken up to be taken by police car to Lerida for questioning. As the mountain passes proved to be blocked by snow, we had to stay for three days in the village, waiting. We were allowed a reasonable freedom of movement and were given excellent wine. Our guards were decent fellows, with whom we were soon on good terms. We had the impression that the Spaniards were beginning to doubt whether their dear friends the Germans were going to win the war after all. And that doubt made them more inclined to be friendly to the Allies.

I noticed that on arrival in Lerida, where we were expecting to be clapped in gaol, the Dutch Consul was able to arrange hotel accommodation for us. Providing we were indoors during the hours of darkness, we were free to go where we liked.

On the third day after our arrival Ubbink and I were called on by Mrs. Crince le Roy of the Netherlands Embassy in Madrid, who showed us evidence that she was empowered to act for the military attaché. She asked us to draw up a written report about conditions and events in Holland and assured us that arrangements were being made to send us on as soon as possible.

Early in January we received permission to proceed to Madrid, and there we reported to Captain Hertzberger at the embassy. He, too, was given a full report of our work.

The Spanish authorities were in no haste to give us permits to go. Towards the end of January we were unexpectedly requested to call at the British Embassy, where we were told to hold ourselves in readiness for the journey to England. Would we be ready to leave the next morning? We were to carry no more than a brief-case containing essential articles of toilet, for we were to leave without the permission of the Spanish authorities, and it was therefore necessary to create the impression that we were missing. We should have to leave the bulk of our belongings at the hotel.

Together with two R.A.F. pilots, we were taken to Seville in a car of the Corps Diplomatique. C.D. cars, flying the British flag, were unlikely to be stopped by the Spanish police. We arrived at Seville at night and were taken straight to the British Consul, who informed us that we were to be smuggled on board a British freighter. The ship was in the harbour and was scheduled to go straight to Gibraltar.

The harbour was well guarded and ships of belligerent nations were closely watched. Nevertheless we got on board, where we were immediately hidden: we spent eight hours in the double wall of a boiler that was not in use. As the boiler next to it was, we came out half-boiled. It was a joy to be back on board ship, for both Ubbink and I had missed the sea more than we had been prepared to admit. On the voyage we met a British destroyer, which escorted us and safely took us to Gibraltar within a couple of days.

There we were met by a captain of the Intelligence Corps who found us lodgings. We were to hold ourselves prepared to board the first available plane for England. At ten o'clock that night we left, and within nine hours made a perfect landing on an airfield near Bristol. It was February 1st, 1944. I gazed round. I had been out of England for eleven months, and what a roundabout return journey I had made.

A sergeant of police immediately separated us from the other passengers. He solemnly addressed us, "Gentlemen, I salute you. I have the greatest admiration for agents who return from operations!" He gave us a regulation salute and asked us to wait for someone from London who was coming to meet us.

We were taken to the station that evening and handed over to a Dutch-speaking Englishman belonging to M.I. who took us to a place near London. There, he said, we could have a rest after our exhausting experiences. I told him I was not particularly in need of rest and that I wanted a talk with my chief, Colonel de Bruyne. Our guide smiled politely. "I'm sorry, but that is impossible for the time being. I have my orders."

We were exceedingly surprised, but not as yet suspicious; we were not, however, left in doubt long. After a day or two we were taken to London for interrogation, and the only people we saw were British intelligence officers. After our interrogation we were taken to Guildford, where our freedom of movement was very restricted. When we went out we had to be accompanied by a security sergeant and we were not allowed to speak to anyone.

After yet another interrogation it was clear that we were not trusted. Ubbink was practically told in so many words that he was working for the Germans. I was utterly taken aback. Good God! I thought. Why must they do this to me? Is this what I risked my life for, time and time again? Is this why I escaped from Haaren prison? Is this why I trekked across four countries, hounded by the enemy?

I wrote letter upon letter of despair to Colonel de Bruyne, and in reply I received little notes telling me not to take it to heart. He and Captain Lieftinck were doing what they could to help us, he added. But I could not help taking it to heart. For days on end Ubbink and I tried to work it out.

"Appearances must be against us, Benny," I said. "They will not believe us, and they have obviously ignored our warnings. I'm sure that, when we escaped, the Germans must have told the English by means of the captured transmitters that we were traitors. And these people have swallowed all that the Germans chose to tell them."

"They still believe it," Ubbink agreed, "unless——"

Indeed: "Unless——" What exactly were we up

against? In the course of one of our interrogations we were told that Van Bilsen, the Tilburg man who had done so much to help us, was a Gestapo man. At any rate he had been a Nazi sympathiser as late as 1941. We were assured that he had been killed, a few months after our escape, by members of the Limburg underground movement.

We could only say that there must have been a mistake. Sometimes the discussions about Van Bilsen became very bitter, because we were indignant at the allegations against this man who had risked his life day after day. I had once had misgivings about him, but had never felt distrust. I felt he was reckless. I had written an article about conditions in England and he had published it, signed with my initials, in an underground paper. I had been afraid that the Germans would be able to find the printers of the paper if they tried, but Van Bilsen had said that my fears were exaggerated.

A second point that the British officers could not understand was that we had been treated rather well in Haaren prison. They had different information from many other prisons and did not believe that there might be Germans who tried unusual methods. In a concentration camp a few miles away from Haaren, several prisoners were beaten to death, but such happenings were extremely rare at Haaren itself.

This situation lasted three months. Interrogations were now being replaced by accusations. In May we were suddenly transferred to Brixton Prison and put in cells alongside common criminals. These incidents added years to my age.

I heard rumours of fighting in Normandy. A second front had been established. For years I had been hoping to be in that. And now I could only look out of a cell window and think of Haaren. There was a solitary tree in the courtyard at Brixton, pale green in the spring sunshine. And as I gazed at it there was a fearful explosion and I was thrown backwards on the floor. A V1 had come down just by the prison. When I regained consciousness I found I could not see, and I began to worry—was I permanently blind? But in a few days there was a slight improvement. I had been taken to the prison hospital, and there, one day, I was visited by Colonel de Bruyne and Captain Lieftinck. They told me they were still doing what they could to get us released. They did not doubt our trustworthiness, but the British security officers did.

A week later we were suddenly set free. Captain Lieftinck came to meet us and took us to Colonel de Bruyne, who welcomed us and expressed his regret at what had happened. I told them that I was prepared to go straight back to Holland to help liberate my imprisoned comrades. De Bruyne seemed to approve of the proposal and said he would discuss it with the British. The next thing he told me was that I had been reduced to the rank of corporal, as my special mission was ended. And thank you very much—rules and regulations, you know.

With tears in my eyes and flushed cheeks I left that office with bowed head, a disillusioned man. Yet we were still fighting the war, and the behaviour of a few must not be allowed to hold me back from doing my duty. I volunteered as a gunner in the Dutch Air Force; I was quickly trained, and late in 1944 went on active service as a corporal gunner with Air Squadron No. 320.

I saw Holland again during the liberation days as we

flew low over the land. It was a sadly battered but a free country.

Forty-eight of my companions in Haaren had been murdered by the Germans in November 1944 at Mauthausen concentration camp. I had, after all, been lucky.

CHAPTER 17

THE QUESTION

"WHERE ARE the agents?" was the question heard on all sides in Holland after the war. The country had suffered as had few others in the last seven months of hostilities, after the failure of the Arnhem campaign. Many thousands of the young men and women deported then were returning from the German prisons and camps. Every day, in the reduced post-war newspapers there appeared long lists of the missing inserted by people who wanted information about a relative or a Jewish friend who had been deported. Sometimes there was an answer; more often silence. Those who returned made a round of sad visits to the relatives of their comrades who had perished in Germany. The frightful truth about the Jews was known soon enough. People who had lost husbands, brothers or fathers in Germany heard in a few months of their fate. But there was no news at all about the Dutch secret agents who had spent a great part of the war at Haaren. Three months after our escape from the prison, three others had managed to break out, and the Germans used this as a pretext for transporting those who remained to Germany where there was less chance of escape. All promises that they should stay in Holland were forgotten from the moment the Nazis realized that the Anglo-Dutch Secret Service had stumbled on the truth. The captured agents were no longer useful. Two of the three who escaped after us were shot without further ado. When the third fell into German hands they did not bother to kill him, and he was sent to Germany with the rest. What had become of them? Only after a year was the truth made known.

On September 6th and 7th, 1944, forty-seven people were murdered by the S.S. in the quarries of Mauthausen concentration camp. Seven of them were British; forty were Dutch agents who had been brought from Haaren. They had been set to work carrying heavy stones up the stairs of the quarry. As they became exhausted the guards told them to fetch lighter stones from the entrance of the quarry. There the S.S. were waiting. Every prisoner who appeared at the entrance was shot down as if trying to escape. On September 6th fourteen men were killed in this way. The following day many prisoners, realizing the intentions of the Germans, presented themselves deliberately at the entrance of the quarry; their life of ceaseless kicking and beatings by the guards had become unbearable. At the end of September 7th the few men left were taken out by the guards and executed.

Eleven other agents who had been taken to Germany with the forty Dutchmen were never heard of again. It is assumed that they have also been murdered.

The Dutch newspapers took up the question of the agents. The questions we had asked each other so often in Haaren, and also later, were heard throughout the country. What had happened? How was it possible that these agents had fallen straight into the hands of the Nazis when they were dropped? Of them all only two men, Hubert Lauwers and Wim van der Reyden, and one woman, Beatrix Terwindt, had survived. Was it true, as had often been suggested in the papers, that these three had betrayed the others? It was known that they wanted a chance to prove their innocence and clear their names.

Then the most dangerous collaborator in Holland, a man who had given information to the Gestapo and was responsible for the death of countless Dutch patriots, declared that he had carried out his betrayal on instructions from the British Secret Service. His name was Van der Waals, a name which in Holland has become synonymous with the word treason, as has Quisling's name throughout the world. The most curious fact was that the British had arrested Van der Waals soon after Germany's collapse, and for some time he had worked for them, even visiting the Russian zone to gather information. Only after bitter protests from the Dutch had he been extradited. Was it possible that the British had deliberately sacrificed a number of Dutchmen in order to divert the attention of the Germans from other more important operations? Many Dutch authorities in such matters expressed this view, and public indignation rose. A Dutch psychiatrist, who claimed that he had been a member of a British spy-ring in Holland, confirmed what Van der Waals said, and added that there had been other British spies working in Holland in the guise of Nazis. The Germans who arrested the Dutch agents were in fact also secret agents for Britain and had arrested the Dutchmen as cover for their real activities. In many newspapers the term "perfidious Albion" appeared. They also published inaccurate and incomplete versions of the stories of two prominent Germans in Dutch captivity. These two men, who had been in charge of the German side, were the wily Gestapo man Josef Schreieder, head of the counter-espionage of the Gestapo, and Colonel H. J. Giskes, officer of the Abwehr, the counter-intelligence department of the army. They both seemed ready to tell what they knew. Schreieder was an unusual member of the Gestapo. He had never been in favour of brutal methods and could prove that he had given instructions to his men to treat their prisoners decently. His orders had usually been followed. Giskes had all the virtues of the German officer and great contempt for the Gestapo. Both had little to hide. They had done their duty with great enthusiasm and it was in their interest to prove that they were not war-criminals. They were the first to tell the story about what Giskes called "Operation North Pole" and what has become known in Holland as the "England Spiel", "The England Game", the name given by Schreieder to this operation. There was absolutely no question of treason, they both said, neither on the German nor the British nor the Dutch side. Early in the war they had got on the track of the British agents in Holland who were transmitting information to England by radio. Giskes and Schreieder each hit on the same plan: to lay hands on one of these transmitters and its operator and use them for their own purposes and in such a way that the British would never suspect that their man was no longer at liberty.

Schreieder was the first to try out the scheme. He had captured the agent Van der Reyden, who claimed that he had not come to Holland of his own free will, that long before the war he had been a member of the Dutch Nazi Party and after his arrival in England the British, having discovered this, had made him choose between being sent back to Holland as an agent and being interned. "If you were treated like this," suggested Schreieder, "you probably have no objection to working for us." Van der Reyden complied, but the British had never answered his messages, and the German failed to grasp that he had been fooled by this former Dutch Nazi, who had told him no more and no less than his chiefs in England had instructed him to do if caught.

[172]

Giskes was more successful. In March 1941 he caught the agent Hubertus Lauwers in The Hague in the act of transmitting a message to England. Lauwers also agreed to work for the Germans. When Giskes questioned him about the security-check, confident that Giskes would not notice that the version he gave him was incorrect, he relied on his chiefs in London realizing immediately on getting the first message he sent for the Germans that he had fallen into their hands. He proceeded to act on this assumption, and when the British answered his message he thought that they had understood the situation and were in turn trying to fool the Germans. But in their following messages they announced that a new agent was to be sent and asked Lauwers to meet him. This was the first unfortunate to fall into the arms of the waiting Germans, who had formed a reception committee composed of Dutch traitors.

Thus Operation North Pole began. It was to continue for twenty months. Only when our message, smuggled out of Haaren prison, reached England more than a year later were no more agents dropped into the hands of the Germans.

This was the story according to Giskes and Schreieder. But points remained unsolved. Why did the British ignore the absence or incorrectness of security-checks? There was the story of Van der Waals, who said that they knew what they were doing. There was also the theory that Schreieder was a British agent who had to produce prisoners to lull the suspicions of German superiors. Schreieder denied this violently. "I am a good German," he said, "and I should be deeply ashamed if I had worked for the enemy." But he himself could not explain why the game had gone on for such a long time and with such success. He and Giskes had discussed the matter often enough and agreed with their superiors that it was "too good to be true".

Schreieder and Giskes and the surviving Dutch agents were taken to England after the war and questioned for months. It appeared that the British authorities had also been puzzled by events and had considered the possibility of treason. After a long investigation the Germans were handed over to the Dutch authorities and no charges were made against them. Lauwers and Van der Reyden were also released after questioning. None of them knew what the British authorities brought to light in the course of their investigations of this affair, which the Germans on their side considered the great st feat of their counter-espionage.

Meanwhile the indignation in Holland grew. Questions were asked in Parliament and in the end a parliamentary commission was appointed to investigate the whole affair. This commission sat for more than two years. It questioned all the survivors of Operation North Pole, all the available Germans who had been concerned in it, almost every Dutchman who could give information. The chairman, Mr. Donker, who later became Minister of Justice, approached the responsible authorities on the British side, who put their findings at his disposal. At last the riddle was solved. The names of Lauwers and others were cleared. Ubbink and I were rehabilitated five years after the end of the war and had a Dutch military decoration pinned on our chests. We knew then that there had been no treason; only inefficiency. We knew then how Operation North Pole could start and how it could continue for such a long time. I understood why I had been treated as a suspicious character, almost as a traitor, when I returned to England, and why Van Bilsen, the man who risked his life for us, had been shot by the Dutch underground.

The Germans had always suggested to their bewildered prisoners that there was a traitor in England, an officer in charge on the British side. The captured agents had reached the conclusion, in their endless discussions in Haaren prison, that a British officer who served in the Dutch section of Special Operations Executive, the organization that sent most of the agents abroad, was the most likely man to be playing this double game. To the relief of many Dutch people, this theory has also been proved baseless. This officer had only joined S.O.E. after the tragedy had already started.

After Mr. Donker's visit to London, where he got all possible help in his inquiries, the Foreign Office issued a statement reviewing the investigations by the British authorities. Although the Dutch parliamentary commission did not agree with all that was said in this statement, it presents a good summary of the case and the British point of view. Here it is:

Statement from the Foreign Office for Dr. Donker, Chairman of the Netherlands Parliamentary Commission of Enquiry

1. During the last year enquiries have been received relating to the evidence put before the Netherlands tribunal concerning the conduct of clandestine operations in Holland and the German penetration of resistance movements. The Foreign Office has, of course, no standing in relation to the Tribunal. However, certain allegations have appeared in the Netherlands Press, and elsewhere, to the effect that the British military authorities, in so far as they were responsible for the conduct of these operations, had other ends in view than those which they declared to the Netherlands authorities. There is not a shred of truth in these

allegations: in organizing sabotage in the Netherlands, and in supporting the Netherlands Resistance Movement, the British authorities were guided by one consideration only—to attack the enemy in those areas where the Allied forces were not in contact with the German Army. In implementing this policy, with which the Netherlands Government-in-Exile were in complete agreement, the British authorities received the wholehearted collaboration of the Netherlands authorities and the devoted services of many gallant Dutchmen.

2. The suggestion that the British authorities departed from the objectives which they had agreed with their Dutch colleagues and, in particular, the suggestion that the lives of Dutch patriots were deliberately sacrificed in the interest of other objectives in the Netherlands, or elsewhere, are both repugnant to His Majesty's Government and the British people and entirely lacking in foundation. In order, therefore, to correct any false impressions which the above-mentioned allegations may have created, the Foreign Office wishes to place certain facts before the Commission.

3. The organization concerned with all these matters in the United Kingdom was disbanded immediately after the war and the bulk of its records destroyed: this has necessarily put serious obstacles in the way of the enquiry. It is of particular importance to note that the actual wireless messages to and from the Netherlands dealing with the day-to-day conduct of the operations were destroyed with the other records. It is impossible now to give the exact number of these messages, but, bearing in mind that similar operations were taking place in other territories occupied by the enemy, there

[176]

could not have been fewer than several hundred thousand of them.

However, it has been possible to check certain of the relevant dates, and the following facts emerge.

4. The resistance activities were regarded and conducted by both sides as joint operations based on the United Kingdom.

5. Communications to and from the United Kingdom were naturally controlled by His Majesty's Government. This was the normal rule, although its rigidity was, to a certain extent, relaxed as the war developed.

6. At the crucial stage in the penetration of the Special Operations Executive Militaire Inlichtingen Dienst (S.O.E.—M.I.D.) operations, that is in March 1942, when the messages from the agent Lauwers, alias Ebenezer, began to arrive without the proper security-checks, the Senior Netherlands Officer, then Colonel de Bruyne, was not in a position to check the texts of the signals received and despatched.

7. The enquiry conducted at the time in Great Britain was necessarily incomplete because no evidence on the German side was then available. But it is conclusively established that the original penetration was due solely to the operations of the German counter-intelligence, and that these produced a chain reaction owing to the system of reception committees which were jointly considered necessary owing to conditions in Holland, especially in view of the highly restricted dropping areas.

8. The most important result of the penetration of these operations was that, as it took place at an early stage, it led to complete German control. An important contributory cause of the penetration, and

particularly of its continuance, was that the omission of the security-checks by certain wireless transmitter (W/T) operators was ignored.

9. Investigations were held at various periods after the original penetration had begun, but in each case a decision was taken to continue the operations. These decisions were reached after taking into consideration the personalities and characters of the agents, and with the knowledge that the security-checks had been proved in other cases to be inconclusive as a test.

10. It was later realized that the decision to continue the operation was mistaken.

11. The controlling headquarters in London were not unaware of these reasons and made repeated efforts both to obtain a cross-check from inside Holland and to discover indications of enemy control in the messages received. All these efforts proved abortive.

12. At the crucial date, which, as mentioned above, was disastrously early in the proceedings, Major Bingham was not in charge of the British side of the section and was not in a position to decide the policy. He himself was opposed to the system of reception committees, and as soon as he took charge (in March 1943) insisted on doing away with it and adopting the more secure system of the "blind drop". Major Bingham was also responsible for ensuring that Dutch officers should be able to examine actual texts of telegrams where appropriate.

13. The various and searching enquiries held by His Majesty's Government into the failure of Special Operations Executive (S.O.E.) operations in the Netherlands during 1942 and 1943, leaving aside

such errors of judgment as may have occurred in the course of their conduct, have not revealed the slightest grounds for believing that there was treachery either on the British or on the Netherlands side.

14. The allegation that British intelligence agents, about whose existence and activities the Netherlands authorities were unaware, were employed in the Netherlands is completely without foundation.

15. For reasons of elementary security the organizations in the field controlled respectively by S.O.E., whose function was to organize sabotage and resistance, and by the Intelligence Service, whose function was restricted to the acquisition of intelligence, were kept entirely separate. Hence it follows that there was no collaboration between the headquarters of these two organizations in the operational sphere and only such occasional collaboration in intelligence matters as was necessary to ensure that each received information of direct interest to itself. When the Intelligence Service received information that the S.O.E./M.I.D. operations had been penetrated, S.O.E. headquarters in London were immediately notified. Such information was not, however, received until May 1943.

16. It is the wish of His Majesty's Government that no facts should be concealed which could assist the Commission in their enquiries. The Foreign Office, therefore, invited the British officers whose names appear below, and who had been responsible for the conduct of clandestine operations in the Netherlands during the war, to meet the Chairman of the Commission in their capacity of private individuals and to discuss the subject with him. They accepted the invitation, and a series of conversations took place in London from the 3rd to the 10th October. These officers were

invited to answer with complete frankness any questions put to them. They were, of course, under no obligation either to appear at all or to make any statements or to answer any questions.

Mr. Laming (S.O.E.)
Major-General Sir Colin Gubbins (S.O.E.)
Brigadier Mockler-Ferryman (S.O.E.)
Colonel Brook (S.O.E.)
Colonel Cordeaux (Intelligence Service)
Mr. Senter (S.O.E.)
Mr. Miller (S.O.E.)
Mr. Seymour (Intelligence Service)
Mr. Bingham (S.O.E.)
Colonel Rabagliatti (Intelligence Service)

There is no need here to recapitulate these conversations, of which the salient points are at the disposal of the Commission.

14th December, 1949.

The disagreement between the Foreign Office and the Dutch tribunal is to be found in paragraph 13. The British ascribe the tragedy to "errors of judgment". The Dutch tribunal speaks in its reports about "serious blunders". The reason for this different evaluation of the events is probably that the British saw the operations in Holland as a part of the whole and generally excellent work of S.O.E., while the tribunal placed all emphasis on the failure in one country. The general of a victorious army takes a different view of the battle from that of the commander of the one company of his troops that was decimated.

Special Operations Executive (S.O.E.), the organization that was set up in England to conduct a new kind of war in the rear of the enemy, developed a bad reputation in Holland. In other countries S.O.E. can boast of great success in organizing the underground resistance against the Germans. In a S.H.A.E.F. report of 1944 it is said that the action of the resistance groups south of the Loire resulted in an average delay of forty-eight hours in the movement of reinforcements to Normandy, and often much longer. In May 1945 General Eisenhower wrote to Major-General Sir Colin Gubbins, head of S.O.E., to thank him for his work. Eisenhower said: "While no final assessment of the operational value of resistance action has yet been completed, I consider that the disruption of enemy rail communications, the harassing of German road moves and the continual and increasing strain placed on German war economy and internal security services throughout occupied Europe by the organized forces of resistance, played a very considerable part in our complete and final victory." This is high praise for S.O.E., which organized these forces.

When one studies the work of S.O.E. one finds that there was only one instance of complete failure: the operation in Holland. The Germans of the counter-espionage in the other occupied countries had few stories to tell about their successes against the British, and even in Holland it was limited, as we shall see.

Considering that the Germans had been preparing their total war for years and could place highly experienced men like Schreieder and Giskes in all occupied territories, and that the British had to start from scratch after their troops had been chased from Europe, the outcome, except in the case of Holland, is not discreditable. Some mistakes could hardly be avoided.

An idea of what S.O.E. really was can be given by drawing freely on a lecture by Major-General Sir Colin

Gubbins on the work of this organization which appeared in May 1948, in the *Journal of the Royal United Services Institution*. After the disaster of the spring of 1940 the British were "up against it". The British Empire stood alone against the Nazis, who were ready to eliminate the last obstacle to world domination. Germany had waged total war, and her success had been greatly assisted, as everybody in the occupied territories knew, by subversive methods long prepared and practised. Many people in England realized that it would be years before an offensive would become possible. But in the meantime one could attack the enemy by unorthodox methods. Special Operations Executive was created to do this: to attack the German war potential wherever possible and to organize the patriots in the occupied territories, where the enemy was lording it with almost unbelievable impudence, creating a hatred and hostility which might be of the greatest possible assistance to the liberating armies when the invasion of the Continent should come at last.

"Here was the problem and the plan, then," as Major-General Sir Colin Gubbins said: "to encourage and enable the peoples of the occupied countries to harass the German war effort at every possible point by sabotage, subversion, go-slow practices, *coup de main* raids, etc., and at the same time to build up secret forces therein, organized, armed and trained to take their part only when the final assault began. These two objects are, in fact, fundamentally incompatible: to divert attention from the creation of secret armies meant avoiding any activity which would attract German attention; to act offensively entailed attracting the special attention and efforts of the Gestapo and S.S. and the redoubling of vigilance on their part. Not an easy problem, but somehow the two had to be done.

"In its simplest terms, this plan involved the ultimate delivery to occupied territory of large numbers of personnel and quantities of arms and explosives. But the first problem was to make contact with those countries, to get information of the possibilities, to find out the prospects of getting local help, and an even more immediate task was to find someone suitable and willing to undertake the first hazardous trip, then to train him and fit him for the job and ensure communication with him when he had landed.

"All contact with occupied territories closed when the last British forces returned to Great Britain in 1940, so the first man to go back to any country had to be parachuted 'blind' as we say, i.e. there was no one waiting to receive him on the dropping ground, no household ready to give him shelter, conceal his kit, and arrange his onward passage, provide false papers, etc. He just went 'blind' and had to use his native wit to establish himself safely and open up communication. His training was, therefore, of the utmost importance.

"And so the first organizational steps were taken—the search for suitable personnel, the setting up of training schools, the establishment of research stations for the production of specialized equipment and weapons, of wireless sets capable of being carried by one man, the production of identity papers, ration cards, demobilization papers etc.; the provision of foreign currency, research into the methods of the Gestapo, experiments in the dropping of specialized stores from aircraft, and so on. A whole host of preparations had to be initiated before the first man could be dropped, and research and development continued throughout the War."

And here are some of the results before the invasion of the Continent:

"FRANCE

    (*a*) The destruction of the Ratier air-screw factory at Toulouse;

    (*b*) The destruction of the power supply arrangements for Le Creusot, the biggest armament works in France;

    (*c*) The demolition of the Gigny barrage on the Saone, holding up German E-boat traffic to the Mediterranean for five critical weeks. This operation was repeated in the following year;

    (*d*) The demolition of Radio-Paris, used for jamming and propaganda;

    (*e*) Innumerable power stations and transformers;

    (*f*) Continuous rail attacks, particularly against supply trains carrying coal to submarine bases.

"BELGIUM

    (*a*) Power stations and transformers destroyed;

    (*b*) Demolition of locks, etc., on main waterways between Belgium and France;

    (*c*) Destruction of high-tension cables and pylons.

"DENMARK

    (*a*) Shipyard sabotage, particularly the yards of Burmeister and Wain;

    (*b*) Fourteen ships sunk in harbour in the nine months preceding the invasion of Norway;

    (*c*) Attacks on railways.

"NORWAY

    (*a*) Demolitions at Orla pyrite mines and destruction of plant;

    (*b*) Demolition of torpedo and submarine oil stocks at Horten;

[184]

(*c*) Destruction of Skefco ball-bearing works in Oslo;

(*d*) Destruction of the heavy-water factory and stocks at Rjukan.

"GREECE

(*a*) Destruction of Gorgopotamos railway bridge;

(*b*) Rail and road demolitions in June 1943, as diversion for Allied invasion of Sicily;

(*c*) Kidnapping of General Kreipe from Crete;

(*d*) Sinking of German shipping in Piraeus."

The second task of S.O.E. was the formation of secret armies which would go into action at the moment of the invasion, or later whenever required. On June 5th, 1944, some hours before D-day, the messages went off calling the French Resistance to go into action that same evening. Immediately the underground armies began their work. Sir Colin Gubbins said:

"Within the first week of the invasion 960 railway demolitions out of a planned 1,055 had been well and truly carried out; similarly with communication and road demolitions; and the fighting behind the lines began. By August, 668 locomotives had been destroyed and 2,900 attacks on railways carried out in France alone. Our embarrassment was then to prevent a premature *levée en masse*, a rising of the French people. In this we were not wholly successful, particularly in the case of certain groups in the South of France who fought too early and suffered heavy casualties before the launching of the operation under Field-Marshal Lord Wilson from North Africa. This swept like a wind through Southern France and up the valley of the Rhone to the German frontier and

hemmed in once and for all the German forces struggling
to escape from Bordeaux and Toulouse and the South-
West of France, before the net should finally trap them
all, as it eventually did. The French Forces of the Interior
came out into the open: thousands flocked to join and
there was no way of stopping them.

"Thus began the bloody battles in the Corréze, in
Vercors and in Savoie which at first involved heavy losses
to the French though producing a valuable diversion from
Normandy, but which three months later saw the F.F.I.
still unconquered. In June 1944 the Germans were
employing 5,000 men against Corréze, 11,000 with
artillery against Vercors, and on 20th July the 11th
Panzer Division wanted in Normandy was still in
Dordogne."

I have mentioned the work of S.O.E. at some length
for three reasons. It is only just to show that what happened in Holland was not the general rule; these remarks
serve also to show how Holland fitted into the rest of the
great scheme of liberation, and in the third place they
give some indication of why the Germans were able to
continue their game for such a long time.

Many of my friends have remarked on the vagueness of
the instructions I received before being dropped in Holland. In prison at Haaren, and later, I often wondered
precisely what form my work would have taken if I had
not been caught immediately. I was told that my contacts
in Holland would instruct me. Giskes and Schreieder
knew indeed the main purpose of my mission, though
this they never told me, of course. Only long after the
war did I learn that my work was part of a large operation
called "Plan Holland".

In the first two years of the war many members of

Dutch underground groups had made the perilous journey to London in order to enlist the support of the Dutch Government for the plans of their particular movement. There was one very considerable organization in Holland, founded by the officers of the disbanded Dutch Army, called "Order Dienst". Its long-range purpose was to prepare to take over at the moment of German collapse and meanwhile to do everything possible to bring the German defeat nearer. Schreieder and his men had succeeded to some extent in infiltrating this big but loose organization, which had members in every corner of the country. Brave though these officers and their followers were, they had too little experience in this kind of work. In May 1942 seventy-two of them were executed: in July 1943 another twenty leading members faced the execution squads. A reason for these catastrophes can be found in the fact that they tried to be active in too many directions at once. They spied on the German troop movements; they committed sabotage; they forged documents for patriots who had to go underground; they helped the hunted Jews to disappear. Nor did they get any encouragement from the Dutch Government in London, some members of which actually considered themselves neutral after the surrender of the Dutch Army in 1941.

Symptomatic of their attitude was the strange case of the Prime Minister, de Geer, who had fled to England with the rest of the Dutch Government at the time of the German invasion. In 1941, nominally on a mission to the then Dutch East Indies, he quickly changed planes at Lisbon and returned to his family in The Hague. Morale improved somewhat when Professor Gerbrandy, a stubborn patriot, was subsequently appointed Prime Minister. He appreciated the fact, which many of his colleagues seemed to ignore, that his country was at war and in the hands of the enemy.

When Professor Gerbrandy visited the British Prime Minister to introduce his new government he made a mistake common to Dutchmen unfamiliar with the English language. Churchill entered the room and the good professor shook his hand, saying: "Goodbye, Mr. Churchill, goodbye." Churchill looked astonished, while thoughts of de Geer's flight probably flashed through his mind, and he grumbled: "What! Are you leaving too?"

But tough little Gerbrandy had no intention of seeing Holland again until the Nazis had been thrown out. His idea of action was to fight, whenever and wherever he could. When Major-General Gubbins, head of S.O.E., decided that the time had come to make use of the Dutch resistance, he received from Gerbrandy ready and enthusiastic co-operation. In France preparations for the invasions were already in train. Now a plan for Holland was to be worked out.

The object was "to organize, instruct and equip groups from the patriot forces in Holland so that they would be in a position to create maximum and vital disruption in rear of the enemy and thereby prevent the movement of reinforcements and reserves when the time would be ripe to do so". A detailed programme involving the blocking of twenty railway sections, the obstruction of fifty-one road sections, the dislocation of telecommunications by cutting the underground and overhead cables and the destruction of aerodromes was drawn up. For the purposes of this plan the country was divided into seventeen zones. The leading organizer was a teacher called Jambroes, who before he fled from Holland to England had already had considerable experience of underground work. Immediately on his arrival in London he had been asked if he would be willing to return to Holland. He agreed to go back and was trained for the work he was to do there by S.O.E.

Jambroes was dropped in the night of June 27th, 1942. "The invasion is on the way," Schreieder reported to his chiefs when he had studied the operational orders of his new prisoner. In so far as it lay in his power to stop it, the invasion was doomed to failure. The secret army that the British wanted, the organization for sabotage, the master plan to come into operation when the Allied troops were nearing the Dutch coast, all would be brought into existence—but only on paper, a phantom organization behind the wireless messages that would be sent to England asking for more and more men and material to be sent over. The only hitch to this exciting prospect was that Jambroes had been told to work with the O.D., the military underground movement, which Schreieder did not dare to contact in the only feasible way, by disguising Van der Waals as Jambroes, as, should this be discovered, his whole plan would be ruined. It was easier to persuade headquarters in London that the mentality of the O.D. was at present unsuited for this long-term work; its followers were too eager for immediate action and were unwilling to wait for that day in the far future when the invasion should start.

All this was explained in a message to London in which Jambroes further asked permission to work alone. When this was promptly given, Schreieder was in a position to set his plot in motion. Day after day messages were sent about the progress of the fictitious organization. When S.O.E. asked whether the time was ripe for expansion to another province a reply in the affirmative was sent, and a few days later fresh agents and material were dropped into Schreieder's waiting arms. Most of these men arrived with vague instructions; they were told the organization which appeared to work so perfectly would brief them on landing in Holland—the S.O.E. was happy to leave the rest to the trusted men on the other side.

When I was dropped on the night of March 9th, 1943, twenty-six agents from Plan Holland had preceded me. They had been sent out to work under Jambroes; they were all in Haaren Prison.

It is easy to see now how this could come about. There was in the first place the question of the security-check. The British authorities had often found that agents who were at liberty forgot their check or used it incorrectly. The same thing happened with their agents in other countries. If they had worked on the assumption that every agent who gave an inaccurate check was in enemy hands they would have broken off contact with many men who were doing an otherwise first-rate job. Eventually the presence or absence of the security-check came to have little significance. The operators in England who decoded the telegrams usually noted the fact when the check was omitted or incorrect. This is what happened in the case of Lauwers, the British calling it "an error of judgment" and the Dutch "a serious blunder".

The British had one stroke of luck. There was in Holland a German called May, who had made a very careful study of codes and checks. He noted systematically what mistakes S.O.E. made, and this information proved of great use to Schreieder and Giskes. If there had been other such specialists in France and Belgium the consequences might well have been disastrous.

In Belgium the Germans did succeed in playing somewhat the same game. One of the S.O.E. agents went over to them, with the result that sixteen of his comrades were dropped into the hands of the Nazis. One of these, Jean Sterckmans, who returned alive from Germany after the war, was arrested by the Belgian authorities because the very fact that he had survived proved him a traitor. It took him months before he could clear himself. Only long after the end of the war did he discover, as Ubbink and I did, what had really happened.

The very nature of Plan Holland helped the Germans to defeat it. In itself an excellent plan, it failed in execution. Schreieder and Giskes always wondered why the British did not expect greater immediate results; but it was in fact the essence of the plan that the underground army should not go into action till the order came from London. Occasionally there was an exception to this rule, when London asked for an act of sabotage, such as the destruction of a radio station. Then Schreieder and Giskes would contrive some excuse or stage some plausible show to satisfy the men on the other side. But in general the chiefs of S.O.E. did not require action and were satisfied with a prompt answer to their messages. The real test of the organization that was being built in Holland would not come until the day when the underground forces should come out into the open.

One Dutchman who was approached in England as to whether he was willing to return to Holland to work in the underground asked whether any of those who had been sent earlier had returned. Learning that the answer was no, this prudent fellow excused himself. Frequently the question was asked why no independent agents were sent to check up on Plan Holland. Undeniably this should have been done. When Jambroes fell into the hands of the enemy the whole organization which he had come to set up was doomed to failure, as, from that point on, the Nazis controlled the arrival of S.O.E. agents and material.

Again the Germans were fortunate in the men they had working for them. At least sixty people were engaged in Operation North Pole: the German Counter-Espionage, the Gestapo who helped to track down the patriots, and their assistants the Dutch traitors. There were also the crews who worked the transmitters and the specialists who questioned the prisoners. Only a few knew all the details of the plot, but many knew something about it. Yet the secret was well kept.

Some members of the Dutch underground had indeed a vague idea of what was happening. In August 1942 Dutihl had discovered that seven radio transmitters which were sending messages to England were being worked by the Germans. He also knew that agents were falling into German hands, but he had not grasped the connection between these two facts. He came to the conclusion that there was a traitor in London, and that he was a Dutchman. He tried to get this information to London through Switzerland, but his couriers were caught in Belgium.

In any case, it is doubtful that his message would have been taken seriously if they had managed to reach London. The Dutch authorities were unbelievably complacent; it would have taken an earthquake to make them see how Plan Holland was really going.

The agent Dessing, on his return to England, found only the most perfunctory interest in the information he brought. Another comrade of Dutihl's, who had made a list of certain agents whom he knew to be in prison, was rebuffed by a Dutch officer in charge of the Dutch side of the operations with the words: "The results in Holland are absolutely satisfactory." Schreieder maintained that the other side would always be more inclined to place confidence in reports of success than of failure. How right he was.

So it would appear that the principal factors of the disaster were inefficiency, complacency, and negligence. There was also the shortage of men really fit for this work. All of us were patriots, ready to risk our lives, but the training we received was really inadequate, especially in the matter of communications. Ubbink had had some experience with transmitters when he started his training, but he was an exception. I was introduced to these instruments for the first time during the training period, as were most others who were to work as wireless operators.

Operation North Pole was the victory of the professional Germans—who laid their plans long before the war, knew exactly what they were going to do and trained their people thoroughly—over the amateurs on our side, the majority of whom set to work full of enthusiasm but with little or no training, so that they had to learn by experience. This cost lives.

But one thing must not be forgotten. In the long run the German counter-plot failed. The aim of the Germans had been to get data about the invasion, but they never found out what they most wanted to know: the time and place of the invasion. In 1943 they actually sent a message to London, purporting to come from a worried agent, who claimed that it would help him to know the exact date and place. In this case, at least, London promptly realized that something was wrong and broke off all communication with this man. One might say that the British missed a chance here to send the man wrong information and so turn the tables on the Nazis. The essential fact remains that Schreieder was foiled in his main purpose.

He was never able to report to his superiors that the enemy were landing at such and such a place at such and such a time. When he captured the operational orders of Jambroes, instructing him to build up an organization in each of the provinces of Holland designed to come into action at the moment of the invasion, his report to headquarters was a shout of triumph. He allowed himself to be fooled into believing that the Allies would land in Holland.

He was mistaken on another point: from April 1943 onwards another organization was sending agents to Holland; they were being dropped blind and they worked successfully. It took him very long to discover that he no longer had the monopoly of communication with England. For us Operation North Pole was a failure; further it cost the lives of many fine Dutchmen who would have been very useful in the period of reconstruction after the war. But it did not affect the course of the war.

Now another matter must be dealt with: our treatment in England after our return. The key to this little drama lies in the figure of Van Bilsen. Ubbink and I must always feel deeply grateful to this man. We know he did excellent work in the Dutch resistance movement, although he made a serious mistake at the beginning of the war. When Holland was invaded he was a police inspector in the town of Breda, from which he fled at the time of the German invasion with a number of refugees into France. When he returned home he had a disagreement with the mayor and was dismissed the service. Then Van Bilsen made his first blunder; he complained to the Germans and was reinstated by the Nazis. He got a post in Vlaardingen near Rotterdam, where he became a member of a police organization which had been founded by the Dutch Nazis. These facts were known in England. In Holland, Van Bilsen was regarded as a collaborator.

Some time during 1941 he came to his senses, realizing that nothing but resentment at his dismissal had led him far along the path of danger and folly. He resigned from the police, broke off all connection with the Germans and the Dutch Nazis, and took a job as porter in a textile factory at Tilburg, where he moved with his family.

At this point he started his career in the underground movement. Was he still secretly a Gestapo-man, or was he now a good patriot? It is hardly surprising that the question was asked. Many cautious men refused to have anything to do with him. Van Bilsen realized that eventually he would have to answer for his activities in the first year of the occupation. He knew well enough that many unsavoury rumours were circulating about him, and for this reason he did many dangerous things—unnecessarily dangerous—hoping in this way to regain the confidence of his fellow-countrymen. People like Vinken, who conducted us to one of our hiding-places, did not know what to think. They were inclined to the view that on the whole Van Bilsen was to be trusted but that his past made him reckless. Vinken received a bad jolt when my article about conditions in England appeared in *De Stem*, an underground paper founded by Van Bilsen. This article was signed with my initials, and had the Nazis seen it it would have led them directly to the works where it had been printed. After this Vinken broke off his dealings with Van Bilsen.

The chiefs of S.O.E. appeared to be fully informed about Van Bilsen's early pro-German activities. They probably took the view that he had turned traitor like the notorious Van der Waals.

In 1943 a photograph of Van Bilsen was published in a Dutch underground paper, with the caption "This Man is Dangerous". A copy of this paper may well have reached England. In any case, the officers of S.O.E. had every reason to be suspicious of us. Our escape from a prison which nobody had managed to get out of before, Giskes' inspired messages that we were working for the Germans, and the fact that Van Bilsen had played an important part in our adventures—all these together were too much for the men of S.O.E. Now we can understand their distrust. At the time it was the most painful shock of all.

Van Bilsen was killed in Venlo, a town on the German border in Limburg, famous as the scene of the Venlo Incident in which the secret-service men Payne Best and Stevens were kidnapped by the Gestapo before Holland was in the war. It was the picture of him in the underground paper which led to his death. He had gone to Venlo for a conference with some underground leaders and was recognized. It was decided immediately that he must not leave alive. Only a few days earlier seven leaders of the Limburg underground had been surprised and arrested at a similar meeting, on information passed to the Gestapo by a man from Amsterdam posing as a patriot. In those days there was no pardon for Nazi agents and no risk could be allowed of his contacting his friends. Van Bilsen was shot down on his way to the station. He lived for a day, and, in the hospital to which he was taken, made it clear that he understood the reason for his murder, always insisting that a great mistake had been made. Had he lived, the work he did in the underground movement would certainly have exonerated him from any charge of collaboration. The underground paper he founded, *De Stem*, is now one of the leading dailies in the province of Noord-Brabant and pays a pension to his widow.

This leads to the last point. Did the Germans ever intend to spare the lives of the captured agents as they always promised to do? There is no reason to believe that Schreieder and Giskes were not sincere in their assurances. But there is plenty of evidence that to their superiors a promise needed to be honoured only as long as it served a purpose.

Schreieder's chief, Dr. Harster, made his views on the subject clear when he testified before the Dutch parliamentary tribunal. Secrecy was essential for the success of the operation against S.O.E. Should the agents be handed over to the military courts their trial must attract unwelcome attention and North Pole become an open secret. It was to the advantage of the Germans not to try the agents, at least not until the game they were playing had come to an end. Schreieder insisted that the agents stay in Holland, as their co-operation was essential to the work he was doing. Frequently dispatches arrived from London which without their help he could not readily understand. An example of this was one about Operation Aramis. It was directed to Jambroes, and Schreieder would have been at a loss had he not had Jambroes and the others at hand to question on the significance of this operation as part of Plan Holland. It took him hours of patient interrogation before he was able to piece together, from the scanty answers extracted from his prisoners at Haaren, the information that Operation Aramis had reference to Jambroes's eventual return to England. It emerged that the chiefs of S.O.E. actually thought that Jambroes should return to England because he had brought his work to a successful conclusion! Now it was not very difficult to fool S.O.E., but North Pole might have seriously miscarried at that moment had the agents been out of reach.

Our breakout made things very difficult for Schreieder. If anything can be said in his favour, it is that he did his best to keep the agents in Holland in spite of the threats of disciplinary measures from Gestapo H.Q. in Berlin. For the time he had his way, as he could show that there was some hope that S.O.E. would not believe our story and would continue to send, if not agents, further material.

But when in November 1943 three more agents escaped, Schreieder was powerless to protect the rest. The cunning which had served him so well against the British seemed to have deserted him. The men in Berlin showed no consideration to their own people who failed them. The agents were removed from Haaren to Assen, to a safer prison in the north-east of Holland. Not long after they started on their last journey.

Two of the last three to escape were recaptured on a tip from the traitor Lindemans, who, without any foundation in fact, has been called the "traitor of Arnhem". They were taken to Haaren and shot "while trying to escape". When the order to execute them reached Haaren, May, the code specialist, telephoned Schreieder to ask for his intervention. "The whole thing stinks," Schreieder replied, "but don't get mixed up in it." Nor did he lift a hand to prevent the executions.

After the war the British authorities found a letter from Hempel, the superior of Giskes, recommending clemency for some of the prisoners. Considering that this man was well aware of the promises made to the prisoners, it reads strangely. Hempel requests a postponement of the trial, which, according to all promises, would never take place. At the same time he sees no objection to the execution of twenty-seven agents who had been solemnly promised their lives.

Here is his letter:

Abwehrstelle Netherlands   In the field, 6–12–43.
Br. N. No. 779/43 gKdos. Leiter III   3 copies
                                            1st copy
Subject: Agents
Ref. WDN Ia 3921/43 gKdos.

To the:
C. in C. in the Netherlands for the attention of General der Flieger Christiansen or his deputy, H.Q.
Dds for the Netherlands for the attention of SS-Brigadier and General-major of the Police Naumann The Hague.

In reply to the above letter it is reported that 9 of the 55 English agents who are imprisoned at present can be made available for trial immediately. The handing of the remaining 46 agents depends on whether or not the "Nordpol" Spiel becomes known to the enemy through the escape of the 5 agents (2 on one occasion and 3 on another). Until this has been ascertained there are the following objections to the immediate trial of the agents:

1. Some of the agents must be available to answer occasional questions regarding the W/T (Wireless Transmitter) traffic.

2. Through court-martial proceeding the number of people in the "Nordpol" picture would become much too large for safety.

3. As they would probably be tried *en bloc* the agents would become aware of the extent of the whole "Nordpol" Spiel. They could then, since some of them

may receive a remission of the supreme penalty because of their collaboration in carrying out the "Nordpol" Spiel, give the game away through passing letters surreptitiously from the prison whilst serving their sentence or by other means. Should it turn out that the enemy knows about the Spiel, then there will no longer be any objections to court-martial proceedings against all the agents. In that case it would only be necessary to ensure that the agents who had been promised a remission of sentence for their collaboration in the "Nordpol" Spiel are treated accordingly. Two of the agents, moreover, would have been set free and made available to the Ast., as the Ast. intends to use them against the enemy. It is envisaged that the position regarding the Spiel will be clear enough by the end of December 1943 to enable a final decision to be made regarding the trial of the remaining 46 agents. A list of the 55 agents, divided into the following four groups, is attached.

I. The first group of 9 prisoners can be tried immediately. They are no longer needed in W/T-Spiele and have no connection with the "Nordpol" case. In this, prospects of pardon have been held out to V.d. Reyden (No. 2) captured on 13.2.42 and Radema (No. 9) captured on 29.5.42) for their collaboration in an earlier Spiel with W/T.

II. The second group comprises 17 prisoners (Nos. 10–26). They were arrested during the Spiel "Nordpol". The objections mentioned in 1–3 above apply to this group. These 17 prisoners come into question for a remission of the supreme penalty, as the execution of the Spiel "Nordpol" was made possible through their collaboration.

III. The third group comprises 27 prisoners (Nos.

27–53). They were arrested during the Spiel "Nordpol". The objections laid down in 1–3 above apply also to this group. In the opinion of the Ast., however, there are no grounds for pardon.

IV. The fourth group (Nos. 54–55) will not be sent for trial for reasons of expediency. Through their voluntary and longstanding collaboration these agents made it possible to start and carry through the Spiel. The Ast. proposes to set these agents free as soon as there are indications that the enemy has become aware of the "Nordpol" Spiel.

With this letter there was a list of the agents divided into four groups:

Group	Surname	Christian names	Arrested
I.	ter Laak	Johannes Herm. Arn.	13–2–42
	Van der Reyden	Willem Jacobus	13–2–42
	de Jonge	Ernst Willem	23–5–42
	Emmer	Jan	30–5–42
	Ortt	Felix Donau	23–5–42
	Brinkman	Allert	14–7–42
	Alblas	Aart Hendrik	16–7–42
	Niermeyer	Willem Johan	6–10–42
	Radema	Evert	29–5–42
II.	Taconis	Thijs	9–3–42
	Ras	Gozewin Hendrik Gerard	1–5–42
	Baatsen	Arnoldus Albert	20–3–42
	Kloos	Barend	29–4–42
	Sebes	Hendrik Johannes	9–5–42
	de Haas	Hendrikus	28–4–42
	van Steen	Antonius	30–5–42
	Parlevliet	Hermanus	30–5–42
	Buizer	Johannes Joh. Corn.	23–6–42
	Bukkens	Joseph	27–6–42
	Jambroes	George Louis	27–6–42
	van Hemert	Gerard John	24–7–42

Group	Surname	Christian names	Arrested
	Beukema	Karel Willem Adr.	25–9–42
	Mooy	Adriaan Klaas	25–9–42
	Frl. Terwindt	Beatrix	14–2–43
	van Os	Gerard	19–2–43
	v.d. Wilden	Willem	19–2–43
III.	Andringa	Leon Theod. Cornelius	28–4–42
	Jongelie	Roelof Christiaan	25–9–42
	Drooglever		
	Fortuyn	Cornelis	25–9–42
	Kamphorst	Peter	22–10–42
	Koolstra	Meindert	22–10–42
	Pals	Michel	22–10–42
	Hoofstede	Jan Charles	22–10–42
	Pouwels	Charles Christiaan	25–10–42
	Steeksma	Horst Reinder	25–10–42
	Macare	Max Humphrey	25–10–42
	Bakker	Jacob	28–10–42
	Dane	Joh. Cornel	28–10–42
	de Kruijff	Arie Joh.	29–11–42
	Kuseler	George Lodew.	29–11–42
	Overes	Herm. Joh.	30–11–42
	v.d. Bor	Klaas	17–2–43
	Braggar	Corn. Carel	17–2–43
	van Hulsteyn	Corn Elisa	17–2–43
	Kist	Jan Christ.	19–2–43
	v.d. Wilden	Piet	19–2–43
	Boogaart	Pieter	10–3–43
	Arendse	Pieter Arnold	10–3–43
	Rouwert	Frederik Willem	22–4–43
	van Uijtvanck	Ivo	22–4–43
	de Brey	Oscar Willem	22–5–43
	Mink	Antonius Berend Laurentius	22–5–43
	Punt	Maria	22–5–43
IV.	Lauwers	Hubertus Math. Gerard	6–3–42
	Jordan	Hendrik Johan	3–5–42

When Schreieder was questioned about this letter he answered that he had had nothing to do with it. It was written by an officer of the Wehrmacht. Giskes suggested that it must be seen as an attempt to save the prisoners from the Gestapo.

If this was the best that the Wehrmacht could do to protect the agents, one need not be unduly surprised at their ultimate fate.

Who was responsible for their deaths? The question has never been answered. The order to murder them was issued in Berlin. The otherwise voluble Schreieder and his superiors in The Hague suddenly became reserved when they were questioned about this.

This is, for the time being, the end of the story. If the men who gave the order to kill the agents are still alive they will keep quiet.

There is nothing more to be said. The survivors who were under a cloud for a long time got some recognition for their work, thanks to the parliamentary tribunal. If the lessons for the future have been drawn from this tragedy these men did not die in vain. That is the hope of the few who escaped.

APPENDIX

By Royal Decree of October 6th, 1950, No. 25

PIETER DOURLEIN

is created a Knight of the Fourth Class of the Militaire Willemsorde for having distinguished himself in action by outstanding deeds of courage, enterprise and loyalty. After having carried out a brave and daring escape from the occupied Netherlands to Great Britain in a launch of limited seaworthiness, for which deed he received the distinction of the Bronze Cross, and after having in Her Majesty's warship *Isaac Sweers* taken part in a number of naval engagements, Sergeant Dourlein, upon his return to England in September 1942, volunteered to be dropped in occupied Holland as a secret agent, fully aware of the great risks and dangers such a course would entail. After a training of sixteen months he was, during the night of March 9th to 10th, 1943, parachuted into Holland in the neighbourhood of Ermelo in the province of Gelderland, having received instructions to act as instructor and organizer in the resistance movement, there to form active centres of illegal resistance, and, moreover, to provide the Military Intelligence Service in London with information concerning the enemy. Immediately upon arrival on occupied soil, however, he was arrested by agents of the German *Sicherheitsdienst* and fell a victim to Operation North Pole which was then at its height, to be incarcerated in the Gestapo prison at Haaren in the province of Noord Brabant, from which, with the aim of warning the Allied secret services and acquainting them with the fatal outcome of their activities, he, together with his fellow prisoner, the secret agent, J. B. Ubbink, escaped during the night of August 29th to 30th, 1943, and, in spite of great risks, dangers and privations, succeeded, through his personal initiative, in making the journey through Belgium, France,

Switzerland and Spain to Gibraltar, from whence he reached England on February 1st, 1944.

Under suspicion of being a German spy, he was arrested by the British Security Service, a suspicion from which he succeeded in utterly clearing himself after four months of severe mental strain, after which he became a corporal-gunner in Air Squadron No. 320, in which capacity he took part in numerous operations against targets in occupied territory, fully realizing that should he, an escaped Allied secret agent, fall into German hands a tragic fate awaited him.

Throughout the five years of war Sergeant Dourlein, in spite of great dangers and tribulations, gave every proof of unbroken courage and determination, of loyal patriotism and undeviating self-denial.

The Secretary of the Chancellery

(*signed*) C. A. VAN ZELEMAN ELDIK

The Chancellor of the Dutch Orders of Knighthood

(*signed*) H. KOOT.

LONDON CALLING
NORTH POLE

by

COLONEL H. J. GISKES

*Former Chief of German Military Counter-Espionage
in Holland, Belgium and Northern France*

The story of the incredible catastrophe in which the
British Secret Service was trapped into sending 54 secret
agents to capture and death and which crushed the Resistance
Movement in Holland.

" True from beginning to end."—*Daily Telegraph.*

"A narrative more dramatic and amazing than any Secret
Service novel you ever read."—*Liverpool Echo.*

" Incredible were it not for independent confirmation."
—*The Observer.*

<table>
<tr><td>*Demy*</td><td>*Third Edition*</td><td>1 5s. *net*</td></tr>
</table>

WILLIAM KIMBER